OFF THE COURTHOUSE SQUARE

A MEMOIR OF MY LIFE UP TO AGE 21

Samuel Templeman Gladding

978-1-61846-090-5

First Edition

Produced and Distributed By:
Library Partners Press
ZSR Library
Wake Forest University
1834 Wake Forest Road
Winston-Salem, North Carolina 27106

www.librarypartnerspress.org

Manufactured in the United States of America

To the history of people and memory of places
now vanished in the haze of time.
May they be remembered and live
on in the minds of generations
yet to come through stories.

Table of Contents

PART I: EARLY CHILDHOOD (THE FIRST FIVE YEARS)

PART II: MIDDLE CHILDHOOD (6–12 YEARS OLD)

PART III: ADOLESCENCE (13—17 YEARS OLD)

PART IV: COLLEGE (18—21 YEARS OLD)

Foreword

You ou meet people in this world who are going somewhere. They are filled with energy and are having fun on their life's journey and, when your paths cross, they share that fun with you. Sam Gladding has been places. He is still going places. He is like a shark that has to keep swimming to push oxygen across his gills, only in Sam's case, the shark is always smiling and cracking corny puns and blindsiding you with wisdom hidden in wit.

Off the Courthouse Square is Sam's prequel. It is a story beginning with an infant who cast off his body cast and fearlessly went forth to see what the world had to offer. He did this first by launching himself and his tricycle off the front stoop onto the concrete below. In the emergency room, he decided that if he was going to go places, there had to be some improvements in his technique.

Sam and I go back to the beginning of time, our time, that is. Were it not for a hill and many trees you would have been able to see the back of the Gladding house from the back of ours. Our families went to the same church; we had the same Sunday School teacher and were baptized by the same preacher at about the same age. The same Little League teams rejected Sam and me. Only a quirk of school districting kept us apart during grammar school days.

It was at Decatur High School where we took note of each other. By then we both had worked our way through what the Counselor in Sam would now identify as Erik Erikson's first four psychosocial stages and were beginning to tackle Don Super's Growth and Exploration stages. Sam would be able to identify and classify where each episode he mentions in the following pages would fall, but in high school we were just two teenage boys who liked each other, shared some experiences, and with typical teenage nonchalance, formed an indissoluble friendship that has spanned sixty years—and counting.

The beauty of *Off the Courthouse Square* is knowing what becomes of Sam. If you are unfamiliar with his accomplishments, then take a moment right now and scan his publications and timeline at the end of this book. But keep your finger here because there's something important I want to tell you, and that is this: Each vignette from page one to the end, considered by itself, is not uncommon. They are plausible, though some teeter at fiction's edge. Some are funny and some are sad. You will find flecks of nostalgia and bursts of precocious wisdom. You will be caught in the vortex of Sam's energy, and, as I warned you, you are bound to groan over at least one pun.

What is important is that all of these unremarkable events happened to one individual who used the experiences to make himself remarkable. There are variations of Emerson's "All life is an experiment." One is that throughout life you are both the scientist and the subject. Sam's early years certainly provided a wealth of data, yet it was data available to most. It took a special spirit to mix happenstance, plans, and dreams to produce the man who wrote this book.

It is revealing to pick out instances where Sam exhibited a counselor's talent long before he ever realized that would be his calling. It is inspiring to consider how his life's story could have been disappointing, but he would not allow it. It is fun, especially when you know the ending turns out so well, to parse and surmise how he did it.

Christopher D. Hunter, D. D. S.
Author, *The Occasional Dingbat*
Otway, North Carolina

Preface

*O*ff *the Courthouse Square* is a compilation of short stories and vignettes that lay out some of the most memorable events in my life growing up in Decatur, Georgia, at the edge of the Civil Rights era. The actions and events in the book are connected to happenings off to the side of the 1918 DeKalb County Courthouse Square, which has now been modified and converted into the DeKalb Historical Museum. During my formative years, the courthouse in the heart of Decatur was where major legal and civic events transpired in DeKalb County. You could not travel through the City of Decatur without literally going around the courthouse square. Churches, schools, residences, and businesses were all within a few blocks of it. Decatur, where two-thirds of the events in this memoir take place, had a population then of around 20,000, much as it has today. It was not as affluent then but most its inhabitants in the 1950s would have described themselves as "middle class" whether they were or not.

The narratives in this book trace my life as a boy and adolescent growing up on Church Street, a street close to and perpendicular to the east side of the Courthouse Square. Outside of my home environment, the two institutions most dominant within my world at the time were the Decatur First Baptist Church and Decatur High School. They were within a mile of each other on opposite sides of the Courthouse Square but on differently named streets—Clairemont Avenue and South McDonough Street. Both institutions were engaged in building character in young people. Each emphasized positive activities and ways of living. They were educational and instructive. Other than these significant places in my fledging years were my interactions in my parents' house, the City of Decatur Cemetery, Clairemont Elementary School, and Glenlake Park. Planned and unplanned activities with my family, friends, peers, and adult leaders influenced and determined my growth, aspirations, and achievements. They also set the stage for my life as a college student, especially at Wake Forest University.

As you read this book, please recognize all of the events happened, although a few have been embellished as Southerners who tell stories occasionally do. The people I describe outside of myself were (and are) real. I have used their complete names in some places and either first names or initials in other places depending on the story. Tragically, Decatur was still living under Jim Crow laws during the era covered here and the separation of and disparity between Blacks and Whites is a backdrop of this book.

I hope you enjoy these stories for it is through writing stories we create; through listening to stories we reflect; and through owning our stories and embracing those of others that we are transformed and experience life to its fullest.

Before My Time

THE GLADDING AND THE TEMPLEMAN STORIES

Before I was a twinkle in the eyes of my parents, there were the Gladding and the Templeman families. The Gladdings landed on the Eastern Shore of Virginia in the mid-1600s. They were hard-working, patriotic farmers, sailors, merchants, and citizen-soldiers who were people of faith and solid citizens. Howell Gladding came to the Shore as an indentured servant and worked his way up to owning land. John Gladding fought for the colonies in the American Revolution and George Washington Gladding was a soldier in the War of 1812 stationed with troops on the Eastern Shore to keep the British from landing there.

As a group, the Gladdings were not among the elite. Rather, they were common citizens who supported democracy, as they understood it. Their only slippage was their loyalty to the State of Virginia instead of the United States in the Civil War. As the historian Shelby Foote explains it in his volumes of Civil War history, it was a loyalty pervasive at the time and not well understood in the twenty-first century. The Templemans did the same as the Gladdings with their loyalties, although George Buckner Templeman of Fauquier County, Virginia, cast the only vote in opposition to secession in his precinct.

Regardless, the branch of the Gladdings that settled in New England were much more prominent than the Gladdings of Virginia. However, the less prominent of the two family lines made substantial contributions to their communities, the Commonwealth, and to the nation.

The Templemans were a more colorful and worldly bunch than the Gladdings mainly because they were not isolated on the Eastern Shore of Virginia. Three teenage Templeman brothers came to Virginia in the 1730s through Maryland as indentured servants after the death of their parents in England. One of the brothers, Edward, had two sons—Nathaniel & James—who became a part of Continental Army under George Washington. Nathaniel became ill during the winter of 1777–1778 and died at Valley Forge, Pennsylvania, during the Continental Army's encampment there. James fought to the end of the war and named one of his sons in honor of Nathaniel. In the 1940s, Samuel Templeman II, my mother's brother, fought in World War II. He was an Army second lieutenant and was shot in the legs as he crossed the Rhine River in 1945. However, he was fished out of the river by his Army buddies and lived to father a family and serve on the Lenoir, North Carolina, city council.

Despite having much in common, such as being English, Virginia colonists, and people with "stiff upper lips," not tending to be emotional, the Templemans were diverse as farmers, merchants, ministers, innkeepers, civic leaders, and teachers. They intermingled with some of the first families of Virginia in Westmoreland County, although none of them achieved the status of the families with whom they socialized. As time went on, some family members settled in other parts of Virginia, particularly Fauquier County.

The World into Which I Was Born

Few people enter the world at an ideal time and my birth was no exception. I was born on the morning of October 5, 1945. World War II had been officially over for about a month and American military personnel were returning home. While the end of the war might seem like an ideal time to arrive on earth, especially in a nation that was on the winning side, there were other circumstance afoot.

My parents, Russell Burton and Gertrude Barnes Templeman Gladding were 35 and 34 respectively. They already had two children—Margaret Northam (Peggy) who was 3 (May 21, 1942) and Russell Burton Junior (Russell, Jr.) who was 13 months (August 17, 1944). While my parents had talked about a third child, family history has it I was unexpected. To make matters more complicated, I was born with dislocated hips. I spent much of my first two years in Scottish Rite Hospital where I had three operations to "wire" my hips back in place. My parents visited on Sundays and brought me a Hershey chocolate bar when I was old enough to eat one. My brother also had dislocated hips and both of us had plaster of paris body casts from the waist down at times. We were later informally described as "heavy Chevys." Since my mother, Grandmother Templeman whom we called "Pal," and my sister, Peggy, could barely lift, let alone carry us, they pulled us around the living and dining rooms of our house in a Radio Flyer red wagon, modified with a platform and a hole for the bedpan under it.

My mother was the oldest daughter of four children of Samuel and Inez Templeman. Her two younger sisters were Inez and Ruth with a younger brother, Samuel II. She was petite being about 5 feet tall and probably never weighed more than 100 pounds. She was attractive with a good figure, a sharp mind and a religious focus as the oldest child of a Baptist minister. What she lacked in size, she made up for in spirit—determination, perseverance, and even a bit of feistiness.

She met my father in 1931 at a boarding house owned by her maternal grandfather, Robert Leonard Barnes, in Richmond, Virginia. She had gone to Richmond after graduating from Salem College to study for a M. A. at Westhampton College—the female campus of then Richmond College—because she could not get a teaching job during the Great Depression. Unbeknownst to her, my father and his brother, Randolph, had rented a room at the house at 3300 Monument Avenue, in exchange for money and help with the yard work. My parents waited three years to tie the knot because of the accidental death of my dad's father and because of my mother's insistence that my dad make a hundred dollars a month before she would marry him. Their wedding took place in November 1934 in a ceremony where my mother's father, Samuel Huntington Templeman, a Baptist minister for whom I was named, walked her down the aisle and then performed the wedding at the Brown Memorial Baptist Church in Winston-Salem, North Carolina.

My mother and her father were close. He died in March 1945 and my grandmother, Inez Barnes Templeman—Pal—came to live with my parents soon thereafter. Thus in October 1945, my mother was dealing with the birth of an unplanned child, the grief surrounding the recent death of her father, and the arrival of her mother into the couple's modest three bedroom, one bathroom house at 957 Church Street in Decatur, Georgia, a city outside of Atlanta. After that came the dislocated hips discovery and the stress that the two youngest children needed operations and hospitalization if they were ever going to walk.

My father was a bit of a contrast but a complement to my mother. He was the third of four children—two older brothers and a younger sister—born to Henry Arcemus and Maggie Lena Northam Gladding. He stood about 5′ 10″ but was thin, weighing around 135 pounds. Like my mother, he wore glasses and had since the age of four because of what was described as a "lazy eye." He had a high school and a business school education. He would have likely gone to college, probably Virginia Tech, had it not been for the Great Depression. His family had made a living as farmers on the Eastern Shore of Virginia in Accomack County since the late-1600s but 18 months into the Great Depression the farm was foreclosed on and the family became sharecroppers for a few years. Free from the constant labor of being a farmer, my father kept his love of the soil by having a large garden—about 1/3 of an acre—behind our house in Decatur. There he grew many of the vegetables our family ate.

As mentioned previously, the ancestors of my father's immediate family had settled on the Eastern Shore in the mid-1600s. In 1945, he found himself as an office worker at the Virginia-Carolina (V-C) Chemical Corporation, a company that made fertilizer, in Atlanta. V-C, for whom he worked 27 years, transferred him from Richmond to Atlanta in 1942. The transfer may well have saved his marriage because my father's mother and his younger sister, Mildred—both of whom my mother did not like—had moved into my parents' apartment in Richmond in the 1930s and the atmosphere in their flat was "uncomfortable." Regrettably, in the mid-1940s, my father's oldest brother, Hilton, who owned a general merchandise store on the Eastern Shore was fighting lung cancer and would die in 1946.

Thus, in addition to dealing with an unexpected birth, hospital bills, the arrival at the house of his wife's mother, three children under the age of five, and stress from his wife's loss of her father, my father was dealing with the imminent death of his oldest brother. Overall, October of 1945 was a bittersweet time for the Gladdings with gains, losses, and uncertainty.

PART I

Early Childhood
(the First Five Years)

When I arrived in the world, I had a birth defect that was described at the time as "dislocated hips," which is now known as "dislocatable" hips. The condition was due to a defective genetic disorder. In addition to the hips, I had a dislocated left elbow and shortness of statue. I was not affected initially by what would later be seen as disabilities, except I had to wear ugly high top shoes in elementary school that were supposed to help my gait.

To monitor my hip situation, I had to have an annual checkup at Scottish Rite Hospital. At the checkup, the surgeon who put my hips back in place, Dr. Hiram Kite, when examining my legs and mobility would inevitably say during our time together "Stand on one leg like a chicken." I had no idea how chickens stood on one leg but I complied as best I could. Later I learned Dr. Kite had grown up on a farm in Virginia.

Overall, I was a happy preschool child who was stubborn—"spirited!" My spiritedness worked both to my advantage and my detriment as time went by.

CHAPTER 1

The Trike, the Porch, the Dare, the Air

GRAVITY WINS AGAIN

One of the situations that ended up disastrously for me at about the age of four was my attempt to tricycle down the front steps of our house. This incident was not entirely my fault. An older boy, Bill Gunn, who lived down the street, persuaded me it would be fun and he even put my trike on the landing at the top of the stairs. Our house was brick and had eight concrete steps leading up to the front door. At the bottom of the steps, on either side were two concrete barrels about two feet high. I had no idea why they were there. In any case, on that summer morning with my trike on the right hand side of the porch landing, I climbed the steps, got on my tricycle and began to peddle. I may have peddled twice but it was probably only once for after the front wheel went off the landing, gravity took over. I do not remember much about the ride other than being surprised as I went over the handlebars and landed on the concrete barrel to the left of the steps.

Screams broke the silence. My mother came—I am sure with a horrified look on her face—as blood flowed from my injuries. It was then off to Dr. Leslie's office where I was patched up and returned home. I spent the rest of the day inside. Amazingly, my tricycle was not damaged but I did not ride it for a week.

CHAPTER 2

The Great Garage Fall

I should have known better than to hang around Bill Gunn after the tricycle accident but he and my older brother, Russell, were friends and so I found myself at times tagging along with them. One early fall day Bill and my brother climbed up a ladder to a storage area in Bill's garage. I wanted to join them but I could not master the stairs on the side of the garage. They were too steep. No problem. My brother and Bill threw down a rope and instructed me to tie it around my waist. I tied it but apparently not well, for when they started pulling me up, the rope slipped around my neck. I was helpless to inform them vocally so I found myself breathlessly reaching new heights. Finally, as I grasped to touch the landing they noticed I was hanging and dropped the rope along with what it was tied on to: me! I am not sure how far I fell—probably around 15 feet—but the next sound I heard was "thud!" I was on my back with my head cracked open like a watermelon. After the initial sound, the stilly, humid Georgia air was filled with screaming as blood oozed out of my cranium.

Mrs. Gunn found me, wrapped my head in a towel, picked me up, and rushed up the street to take me to my mother, who had already been indirectly informed something bad had happened as my brother rushed into the house minutes before with the words "I didn't do it!" At Dr. Leslie's office, the cracks in my skull were sewn back together. I had the stitches from the adventures for a few weeks and sported a red rope burn around my neck as well. I remember Pal, saying to me that my head would heal before I married. She was right but sometimes my wife wonders if my head should be examined once more.

CHAPTER 3

Trees, Vines, and Leaves but No Tarzan

I climbed trees when I was growing up. I especially liked to swing from the vines of the trees on a hill down the street. I pretended to be Tarzan! Tree vines were great fun to swing from and trees were where birds, that I was fascinated with, lived. I even started a feather collection.

One day I swung from a vine and it broke when I was in mid-air. I came down hard on my back—thud! The wind had been knocked out of me but not my spirit for adventure. I lay on the ground breathless and still wondering what had happened to my body. Finally, I slowly got up, took some deep breaths, and walked slowly and carefully home. I did not tell anyone and the next day I went swinging from the vines again. It was an obsession! I was "king of the down the street jungle"— just not Tarzan!

I do not know why but during this same period on a spring day, I decided to pull the leaves off a small Dogwood tree in our side yard. It seemed like fun at the time. The enjoyment ended though when my father arrived home from work. He was not happy with the tree or me. I remember him asking me why I had pulled off the leaves. I had no answer and he had a switch. I need not describe what happened next. I have not pulled a leaf off a Dogwood since.

CHAPTER 4

Lazarus the Chicken

I barely remember my family keeping chickens. I was probably around the age of three when they got rid of them. While the chickens left our property for good, stories about them remained. The most notable of the tales was of a chicken named Lazarus. She was one of several chicks that were chewed up when rats got into the chicken coop one night. The next morning my father piled up the bodies of ones that had been killed. However, one he thought dead was not. She got up, walked around, and was nursed back to health. She became known as Lazarus as in the Biblical story of the man Jesus raised from the dead.

The chickens at our house were not pets and regrettably, Lazarus became Sunday dinner one day when we had guests. Unfortunately, my brother had become fond of the chicken. He was shocked at what happened and refused to eat dinner that day. I felt sorry for him and Lazarus. I think that in retrospect my parents and Pal, who decapitated the poor fowl, felt bad, too.

CHAPTER 5

Lighting Fires and Divine Retribution

No one at age four should be considered a pyromaniac. However, if the age limit had been lower when I was growing up, I would have fit into that category. I loved seeing fires burn and had a hand in setting a few. Once I almost burned down the neighbor's garage. I would find matches on kitchen stoves and in drawers and off I would go to burn pine straw and leaves.

I am not sure how long my fire-burning phase lasted but I distinctly know when it ended. It was a Wednesday night and my father was getting me dressed for church services. Earlier that day our puppy, Tippy, had been killed in front of our house after I set a fire. I thought it was divine retribution and I was being punished for my actions. I promised my father I would never light another fire and I did not . . . until I became a Boy Scout.

CHAPTER 6

Early Neighborhood Friends

I had two friends in the neighborhood about my age: Pat Hanes and Alan Bradley. I saw Pat more because she lived closer. We apparently played well together. Pat and I talked about how we thought dogs were boys and cats were girls. We spent considerable time watching goldfish in a pond in her parents' backyard and observing an older man, who regularly walked up and down Church Street, dressed in a brown suit. He seemed mysterious because we did not know where he lived. We called him "Mr. Onion Picker" because he would "pick," that is, pull, wild onions out of people's front lawns. Our relationship was placid.

Alan and I were just the opposite. We were not nearly as talkative or as observant when we were together. Instead, we were energy in motion, climbing on rocks in his backyard, playing tag, making sticks into guns for shootouts, exploring nearby woods, and venturing into the rolling hills of the Decatur Cemetery. Together, we were unfocused and a bit wild.

Pat and Alan were my main playmates until the age of five. Each had a distinct effect on me. I was completely different in how I behaved in their presence. My interactions with others continued to vary, as it had with them, after they moved away although I did not realize it at the time.

CHAPTER 7

Two Gun Pete from the Toilet Seat

reschool children are silly; at least my brother and I were when we played some of our games. We played hide-and-seek, tag, checkers, as well as cowboys and Indians. For the most part we were like children everywhere, especially boys. In one case, though we were a bit "off the bubble" in creating a name for a villain we pretended to arrest as the "good guys" who drank sarsaparilla instead of whiskey.

We had Blackjack Bob, Terrible Tom, Awful Alan, and Naughty Nick. However, the worst of our outlaws we named Two Gun Pete from the Toilet Seat! How we came up with the name for this hombre or what his specific crime was have long since faded but when we were at our silliest, we would personify the bandit and say "I'm Two Gun Pete from the Toilet Seat." Just saying the name of our character was as bad as it got as we broke into laughter. Bathroom humor is not a novelty with preschool children. It simply had a different way of being expressed with the Gladding boys.

CHAPTER 8

Milk Bottle Bottoms

In my preschool days, the milkman delivered dairy products to our front door. Milk came in wide neck glass bottles. Because of the wide necks, the empty bottles were not hard to carry from the kitchen to the porch landing. I did it frequently. However, one day I tried to carry too many at once, too many being four bottles. All seemed well until I tripped and almost fell down. As I stumbled, I heard the sound of glass breaking. Looking at the neck of the bottles, I noticed they were fine and I started walking forward again only to hear a crunch beneath my foot. Two of the bottoms of the bottles had broken.

What seemed okay from the top was not. Reality had appeared at the bottom of my chore in a shattered form. Ouch! The immediate and most pressing aspect of this experience was having to explain what happened to my mother. The long-term result was my becoming more careful.

CHAPTER 9

Ants, Fireflies, and Bees

nts, fireflies, and bees all played a prominent part in my early childhood. I was fascinated with them and I am afraid a number of ants were ground back into the Georgia red clay because of me. I remember catching fireflies in a jar and keeping them through the night while my siblings let theirs go. Unfortunately, every time I kept my fireflies overnight they died even though I put grass in the bottom of the jar for them to eat. I learned the hard way that grass is not a firefly food.

I was also fascinated with bees. I captured honeybees and bumblebees in mason jars. I usually let them go. When my parents took us to the Smithsonian in D.C., I stayed and watched the honeybees in their glass plate hive rather than go with the rest of my family to see Alexander Graham Bell's first phone. I think the bees were more interesting, at least to me at the time. They had a buzz on! However, I have seen through the years that phones are just as fascinating and they now, like the bees, have cells.

CHAPTER 10

Sunbeams and the Story Hour: Religion by Song

When I first started tying my shoes in the sunlight on the black linoleum floor of the bedroom I shared with my brother, I noticed in the sunlight there were particles. Most likely, they were specks of dust. In my mind though they were sunbeams and came directly from the sun along with the light. At about the same time, our church put my peers and me into a group called the Sunbeams. The Sunbeams were preschool children who met on Wednesday nights while the adults were in Bible study and other meetings. The group had its own song with a catchy tune. The words are below.

"Jesus wants me for a Sunbeam to shine for him each day/
In every way try to please him at home, at school, at play/
A Sunbeam, a Sunbeam, Jesus wants me for a Sunbeam/
A Sunbeam, a Sunbeam, I'll be a Sunbeam for him."

In addition to being a Wednesday night Sunbeam, as preschool children we were enrolled in The Story Hour on Sunday nights. Again, there was a song with a positive message and a catchy tune. The words were:

"Every Sunday evening to the church we go/
For the happy story hour and we love it so/
The story hour, the story hour, the happy story hour/
We'll sing, and pray and read God's Word in the happy story hour."

When I look back at how religious I was at an early age, I attribute a good deal of it to being a Sunbeam and attending "The Story Hour." I was a lyrical convert.

CHAPTER 11

Christmas Lights and Third Hand Bikes

My first memories of Christmas are not about toys or a tree. They are about lights. I was a bit over age three when my father brought out strings of multicolored lights one cold Saturday morning. I was immediately attracted to the bright colors of the bulbs and he asked me to help him test them. There were probably eight strings. As he sat in a chair next to an electrical outlet, and I sat beside him on the floor, he plugged in the light strings one at a time. If a string lit up all the way, he asked me to put it in the "good pile." When a string did not light up, he said we would have to test it further by screwing in a replacement bulb for the one that did not work. Since he never knew which bulb had died, he had to screw in systematically new ones a bulb at a time. I held either a new bulb or a replacement bulb in my hand. Throughout the process we exchanged bulbs until we found the bad one. While I had liked the strings of bulbs when they were dormant, I delighted in their bright colors when they were lit.

Other memories of Christmas are of getting a tree and setting it up including stringing it to the door; throwing aluminum "ice cycles" on the tree; and shaking presents to guess their contents before the magical moments of Christmas morning. I received nice gifts from my parents that were modest because of my dad's income. The presents I liked most were not clothes.

Probably the best one ever was a third hand bicycle my parents gave me around age seven. My father had gotten Mr. Jenkins at the bike shop up the street to recondition the bicycles he and my mother gave my brother, sister, and me to where they looked like new. I did not know they had been refurbished. It did not matter. I learned to ride on the sidewalk parallel to Church Street and found in the process a form of transportation on two wheels that opened up the City of Decatur for me.

CHAPTER 12

And the Goblins are Going to Get You, If You Don't Watch Out

Like most preschoolers, I occasionally had a bad dream. The world was big and could be frightening. Whenever I had a nightmare or envisioned something terrifying in the dark, I quickly got up and made my way to my parent's bed where I would find a place in the middle of two warm and sleeping bodies. Sometimes, my dad would play "Leo the Lion" with me in the morning when I awoke and I would feel better yet for it was only a game and I always won.

To counter some of my fears around Halloween, my mother suggested I dress as a Goblin on All Hallows Eve. I had no idea what a Goblin was but I knew it was scary. She made me a costume and I went Trick or Treating. The next year, she suggested the same costume since I had not grown much. I questioned whether people would recognize me from being a Goblin the year before. She assured me they would not. Therefore, I wore a Goblin's costume two years in a row. My mother was correct. No one noticed.

I do not remember the costume, what I looked like in it, or much about Halloween in my preschool years, except occasionally people gave me an apple instead of candy. I am grateful my parents helped me overcome fear by being comforting at night and making me a costume where I could pretend to be scary and not be scared. Of course, wrestling with Leo the Lion was also helpful in becoming braver . . . and it bonded me with my dad!

CHAPTER 13

Riding the Hump in a Car Named the Dream Boat

Our first car was a 1950 black Chevrolet. My father took a bus to Gainesville to pick it up and drive it back home because he could get a better price for the car in doing so than had he bought the car in Atlanta. We named the car "the Dream Boat," which was a misnomer if there ever was one because it traveled on land not water. It was the only car we ever named. The Dream Boat took us many places including visits to relatives and friends around Atlanta, North Carolina, and Virginia.

The only problem I saw with the car as I was growing up was the hump in the floor that was very prominent if you were sitting in the back seat. I am not sure why it was there. I have heard everything from it held the body of the car together to it was a casing for the exhaust system pipe. Regardless, it was well defined and rose just high enough, four plus inches, to where those sitting in the middle of the back seat could not put their feet down on the hump without their knees coming up to their chest. In other words, you had to put your legs on one side of the hump or straddle it. I always had to sit in the middle and ride the hump as a child since I was the youngest and smallest of the Gladding children. I straddled the hump most of the time. It was uncomfortable and I envied my brother and sister who each had floor space as well as a window.

Years after the Dream Boat retired to a junkyard pasture, my parents talked to me one evening about how I was always alert on trips while my siblings slept. They seemed to compliment me, for noticing the scenery on our trips, like the Burma Cream Shave signs or the young men out marching in a military parade as we passed the Clemson campus. I started to tell them it was because I was riding the hump and could not sleep. Instead, I just soaked in what praise I could and told them I thought trips in our first car had been interesting and educational. The truth was since I had to be awake, I decided to enjoy the ride, see everything, and learn in the process!

PART II

Middle Childhood
(6–12 Years Old)

For me middle childhood began with the start of school, or actually a month later since I was not six until early October. Kindergarten was not a part of public education in the 1950s but an expensive, private option. My parents could not afford it so I did not attend. I would have been better prepared educationally had they had the means.

Like many in middle childhood, I had more energy than sense at times. Life was uneven and consisted of playing sports, taking up dares, exploring beyond the immediate neighborhood, making new objects, interacting with pets, learning about life and death, engaging in fresh hobbies, finding my strengths, realizing my limitations, going to school, and in the end discovering girls. My emphases were similar to what most boys of my era experienced although my journey during these years had unique fluctuations, deviations, and outcomes.

CHAPTER 14

"Cool," "School," and the First Grade

I have a difficult time speaking English, let alone another language. It is due to what is known as a Central Processing Disorder. In my case, I have auditory discrimination problems. I do not hear distinct sounds—at least English letters or words that might sound similar, such a "ch" and "sh," but are uniquely different. This disability appeared most dramatically in my life the night before I was to enter first grade. My parents were flabbergasted I could not pronounce the word "school." I told them repeatedly I was going to "chool." They were not "chilled out" with my announcement or pronunciation.

I am still not sure why they let me go. I lacked more than a month of being old enough, was small, and immature in more than my language development. They could have held me back. I struggled with first grade but passed and learned more than what may have appeared on the surface. The summer between the first and second grades, my parents worked with me on remedial reading and pronunciations. It was not "cool" but rather an extension of school. It helped.

CHAPTER 15

Thompson, Boland, & Lee

RADIATION FEET AND PRESENT TREATS

In my elementary school years, my mother would take my siblings and me to Thompson, Boland, and Lee, a shoe store in downtown Atlanta. When we arrived, we rode the elevator up to the second floor, which I assume was the floor for kids' shoes. There, the same sales clerk, who was friendly and yet down to earth, always waited on us. My favorite part of the process was looking at my feet under the x-ray machine to see how crowded or roomy my toes were at the end of my old shoes or new ones—when we bought a pair. In the machine, I could see the bones in my feet and like a child of almost any age; I thought the view was fascinating! However, I continue now to be surprised my feet do not give off a green glow due to all the radiation I absorbed in the process of looking at them then!

Another nice feature about Thompson, Boland, and Lee was they sent you a present on your birthday. When I was eight, I received a small flotilla of five wooden sailboats. It was a nicer present than I received from my parents that year. I played with the boats in the bathtub for a number of weeks before they became waterlogged. I am astonished I did not eventually join the Navy or become a sailor when I became of age.

CHAPTER 16

Picking up the Paper

In the third grade, I was placed in Mrs. Isabel's class. She was as strict as an Army First Sergeant and had a white streak through her dark hair which she saw as a beauty mark. She was nice to me and I liked her class even though I was not her top student. One day she gave the class a desk assignment. As I was working on my paper, she passed by, stopped at my desk and pointing to a piece of paper on the floor said: "Sam, is that yours?" I looked down, saw the paper, and replied "No ma'am, but I'll pick it up" which I proceeded to do.

Suddenly, it seemed like the earth stood still as Mrs. Isabel said in a rather loud voice, as if she had a bullhorn: "Class, did you hear that? Sam just said he would pick up paper that was not his." She went on to talk about virtues and doing things for others. I was amazed because I did not think I had done anything special. I still do not. However, on that occasion, I did—at least in the eyes of Mrs. Isabel. It must have affected my later behavior because I still remember it vividly even though I do not constantly scan the environment for loose paper to pick up.

CHAPTER 17

Happy, the Cocker Spaniel

few years after Tippy was killed, my family bought another cocker spaniel. We named him "Happy." I am not sure why—maybe we were happy to get him or the name just seemed to go with "Gladding." Regardless, Happy seemed to do fine with our family for a while. I could even lay on him, as if he was a pillow, and watch television. However, Happy got into the habit of running away by digging under our backyard fence. My brother and I chased him through the cemetery and through neighbors' backyards on a number of occasions. My father fixed the fence but Happy was smart and found ways to escape.

One day Happy found his way out and despite looking everywhere and asking, we could not find him. A few days later, I was walking home from my third grade Cub Scout meeting when I spotted a black and white cocker spaniel lying still under an old bridge near Glenlake pool. I knew right away it was Happy and that he was dead. Nevertheless, I made my way down to where he lay. I was right. When I touched him, he was cold and did not move.

When I arrived home, having broken out in a run, I told my father I had found Happy and explained he was dead. My parents drove me down to the bridge and there my father gently put Happy into an old fertilizer sack, which was the only burial cloth he had readily available. We brought Happy home and buried him at the edge of the garden. It was a sad occasion with many tears. It gave me a close-up taste of the lifeless nature of death.

CHAPTER 18

Getting Saved

BEING BAPTIZED

If there was one obsession Baptists of my childhood were known for, it was getting people "saved." The pressure was on from an early age. Being saved meant professing Jesus as your personal savior and being baptized, i.e., dunked—"immersed"—in the Baptistery before the entire church congregation. My brother and sister preceded me in this ritual but I do not remember when. Regardless, around age 7 I made my profession of faith to our minister, Dr. Hall, a rather tall, friendly, and balding Mississippian with glasses that made him appear scholarly. He then told my parents and arrangements were made for my baptism.

On the night of the event, I went to the men's dressing room above the baptistery and changed into a long white robe that had been laid out for me. I put my street clothes in a locker and kept on my underwear, which was a necessity if something unforeseen happened—what we would call today "a wardrobe malfunction." There were several people of various ages being baptized that night so I had company in the dressing room. Dr. Hall came into the room about 15 minutes before the service and rather than change clothes, he took off his suit jacket and proceeded to put on waterproof hip boots, aka "waders," as if he might go fishing or duck hunting, both of which I later found out he did on occasions. After that, he descended the stairs into the baptistery.

When my time came to be baptized, I descended the same stairs into the water, held my breath through pinching my nose as Dr. Hall had told me to do, and he immersed me and then lifted me up with the words "Raised in Christ through faith." Even though I was young, the ceremony was meaningful. I felt good and I know my parents and Pal were proud. My siblings did not say a word though. I do not blame them. What can you say if you are a child on such an occasion? Fist bumps and high fives had not been created.

CHAPTER 19

Will Lee, Jim Crow, and Racial Poverty

The South I grew up in was blatantly segregated. Jim Crow laws ruled society and the Ku Klux Klan was active, especially outside of cities like Decatur. Yet Blacks and Whites spoke to one another and worked for or with each other within the confines of the written and unspoken rules of society. My first exposure to this interaction came during the springs when my dad hired an older Black man to come plow his garden. Will Lee was his name. Each year he came to our house around late March or early April riding in the wagon that his mule pulled. At first, his journey was short because he lived in a Black settlement up Church Street between the Decatur Cemetery and the First Methodist Church. However, later he and his community were forced to move about 3 or 4 miles south of the city limits. Therefore, when he came to plow his mule-driven wagon inevitably had a number of cars backed up behind. Neither Will nor his mule seemed too concerned. Of course, the mule had blinders on and Will was focused on the road.

It took most of the day to plow the garden. My mother would always fix Will a hot lunch, which she served him as he sat at our breakfast room table. I thought it a bit odd that anyone would want a hot lunch since I always ate peanut butter and jelly sandwiches for the noonday meal.

On several occasions, my father took my brother, sister and me to Will's house when he rode out to ask Will to plow his garden. Will's house did not have a phone and so going to see him directly was the only way my dad could employ him. Will lived by himself although I had the impression he had once been married and had grown children. His house was well below modest. It was a work in progress. The walls of his main room were covered in newspaper probably for insulation. He had a bedroom off the main room but I think his bathroom may have been a privy outside. The only other things I noted were a potbelly stove for heating and cooking and Kerosene lights.

As a young child, I thought Will's life seemed neat. Now I realize how poor he was. His world was confined. He had virtually no hope of rising above where he was. I am not sure he was content with his life, yet, I think he was accepting because he did not have a choice. I am sure he was glad to get jobs like the one my dad gave him. I wish it could have been different. I am sure he did, too.

CHAPTER 20

Making Clothes and Melodies

While my father was an expert gardener and seemed to be able to grow any kind of vegetable or flower, he was somewhat a klutz with tools. My mother, on the other hand, could have made a living fixing furniture, wiring a house, or any handyman chore, if women had been allowed to do such work back then. Not only was my mother skilled with a hammer, she was a wizard with a sewing machine. She bought patterns and fabric and made shirts for my brother and me as well as made dresses for herself and my sister. I have to wonder whether my mother did this work during my elementary school years because she wanted to or whether she did it because we did not have money to buy these items in a store.

Regardless, one summer day my mother took a break from sewing and played some records from the 1920s and 1930s for us. The two I remember best were "The Preacher and the Bear" and "Down among the Sugar Cane." The preacher and the bear was about a preacher who went hunting on a Sunday morning even though it was against his religion. On his way returning home, he met a "great big grizzly bear." After climbing a tree to escape the bear and literally going out on a limb his prayer was:

> "Hey lord, you delivered Daniel from the bottom of the lion's den
> You delivered Jonah from the belly of the whale and then
> The Hebrew children from the fiery furnace
> So the good books do declare
> Hey lord, if you can't help me,
> For goodness sake don't help that bear."

I thought the song absurd but funny and somehow in my mind I could see the preacher praying while the bear waited.

The chorus to the other song was also clever. I had never seen sugar cane but I could picture it in my mind. The lyrical refrain went:

Little stars are winking
Winking' in the sky up above
We know what they're thinking
While we're making love, they're jealous!!
There'll be oodles of kisses
More than I can explain
When I'm walking with my sweetness
Down among the sugar cane.

Those summer days are indelibly etched in my memory. The combining of my mother's skills with the music and lyrics of gifted song writers wove their way into the depths of my mind.

CHAPTER 21

Scrolling, Rolling, and Rubber Banding

BIBLE VERSES IN A NEW FORM

When I was nine, I used to make scrolls. First, I would find a couple of straight sticks that had fallen to the ground from the two water oaks in our front yard. Then I would tape together some paper from one of the notepads in our house. Next, I would write a few Bible verses on the notepads, usually the Ten Commandments or a few verses from the New Testament like the Beatitudes. Finally, I would roll the scroll up, put a rubber band around it, and give it to my father. He would accept the scroll and occasionally I would see it in one of the cubbyholes of the desk in the corner of our living room.

I am not sure how many scrolls I made or why I made them. We must have been studying them in Sunday School. I stopped making the scrolls as spontaneously as I started. I think going out to play won out. I am glad I quit. I was not a good scroll maker. Besides, my father was running out of cubbyholes.

CHAPTER 22

The Littlest Angel

A ROLE THAT WAS LESS THAN DIVINE

There is a reason I am not a professional actor. It has to do with the production of the annual Christmas drama at Clairemont School when I was in the 4th/5th grade combination class. The traveling drama teacher decided that year—1954—the play would be "The Littlest Angel." The lead role was between a second grader and me. I got the part because I was older and the second grader could not sit still for the tryouts.

Almost every day leading up to the production, I was whisked out of my math period and onto the stage to practice. I did not have many lines but I had I had a number of behaviors to act out. The drama instructor was impatient for me to be "off script." As the day of the performance approached, my mother made me a costume while the school furnished the "halo" with plenty of glitter. I did fine in the play but got way behind on math. Hollywood never called and I was never asked to be the lead in another play. Being an angel was less than divine and never led me to consider living in Los Angeles!

CHAPTER 23

The Rescued Kite

In the fourth grade, I took up flying kites. They looked cool up in the sky and they were easy to assemble. My first kite was one I rescued. I chased it down the hill from Clairemont School after the string it was on broke and the boy who was flying it gave up trying to save it from the wind and its freedom. However, the kite, which everyone thought was gone forever, got caught in the upper branches of the apple tree in our backyard. Had it gone farther, I would have let it. Yet, it seemed like a kite I might be able to release so it could have a home and fly again. Therefore, I climbed the tree and tried to reach it. My father was home and came out of his garden to "spot me" should I fall somewhat like coaches do for gymnasts. Being small and light, I was able to climb high, grab the kite by its tail, and manipulate it in such a way that it fell to the ground.

My dad picked it up and assured me, it was not damaged. Days later when I obtained some string, I flew it in the cemetery behind our house. It was a good kite and after it wore out, I saved up and purchased another one.

I sometimes wish I could soar like a kite. Alas though, I was grounded then and remain so today.

CHAPTER 24

Sunday Dinner &
Armchair Playhouse Theatre

S undays were a day of rest for the Gladdings. Paradoxically, they were not. I do not think my mother worked harder on any other day of the week. Frequently, she would start preparing the Sunday noontime meal on Saturday, such as cutting up the chicken. At times on Sunday, Pal would help her as would my sister, Peggy, or my father. However, the majority of the work fell on my mother's shoulders for Sunday dinner, which can only be described as a feast.

Having a large Sunday dinner in the South was quite common in the 1950s and 1960s. Our dinner, which was typical for the times, consisted of fried chicken including the liver, butterbeans, pickled pears or peaches, rice and gravy, biscuits, ice tea, often tomatoes, and various other fruits and vegetables in season. The good china and silverware were always used, which meant more work cleaning up. My brother, Russell, and I usually set the table or put the chairs around it but many times we were doing something else like playing pitch and hit in the back yard. On several occasions, probably 3rd or 4th grade, I remember playing a game of baseball in the backyard with Russell, my dad, and Peggy. It was during those games when everyone noticed I batted left-handed, which they tried but failed to correct. Russell always was the star in our backyard games but since it was all in fun, no one became upset about his abilities to hit and field a baseball.

Usually, about an hour after coming home from church, around 1 p.m., we all sat down around the heavy oak table in our dining room and ate. Sometimes, we watched Armchair Playhouse Theatre. The movies starring Mickey Rooney and Judy Garland were the ones I most enjoyed. I wanted to be like Mickey Rooney when I grew up. He had fun and always got the girl—Judy!

After the dishes were cleaned and put away, my parents would lay down on their bed and rest, often taking a nap. My siblings and I found other things to do quietly, besides go swimming or to a movie, which were forbidden. At around 6:30 p.m. we headed for church and Baptist Training Union (BTU) and Sunday night worship.

I fondly remember Sunday noontime dinners. Sundays, as a whole, were a mixture of religious sermons, strict rules about behavior, and some social times with peers at church. The pattern was continuous, just like a "test pattern" on television after midnight back then.

CHAPTER 25

The Thrill of the Backyard Hill

Our backyard on Church Street was flat but at the end of the lot was a steep hill. In the 1940s and early 1950s, there was a white painted arbor in the front part of the backyard where my siblings and I played and where my parents once thought a snake had bitten my brother. It actually turned out to have been a mosquito bite. The arbor was torn down and a fence put up after we acquired our first dog "Tippy."

Beyond the arbor was my father's garden where he raised over 20 kinds of vegetables. Throughout the backyard were some fruit trees: apple, peach, and pear. I am sure my father talked the pear tree into producing pears when he told it one late summer day he would chop it down unless it bore fruit the next season.

Returning to a focus on the hill, I remember it being straight up— at least 150 feet. It had a few trees and some shrubs on it to hold the red clay soil. A few lizards also inhabited its terrain. My parents cut steps into the hill after they stopped raising chickens and the chicken coop below it was torn down. The top of the hill was flat for about 20 or 25 feet. Beyond that there was a hedge and a slight rise of about three feet, which was covered in kudzu. Beyond the kudzu was the City of Decatur Cemetery. My father joked on several occasions that we had the quietest backyard neighbors in town.

The hill played a part in my childhood on two occasions. The first was when I was about 11 years old. I took my father's hand plow up to the top of the hill and plowed three rows in the dirt, which was very poor soil. Within each row, I planted corn, which came up and matured. With the soil being so poor, the yield was rather pitiful. The stalks were short, maybe two feet at most, and the ears were the size of a pocketknife. When I "harvested" my crop, I left it on top of the hill. It was too puny to show anybody. The kudzu behind the hedge had a better growing season than the corn.

The second time the hill came into my life was as a teenager. My brother and I received .22 caliber rifles one Christmas. I cannot believe my mother approved of the gift since she hated BB guns. On a number of afternoons, Russell and I would shoot at cans. If we missed the targets, the bullets simply went into the hill. We were restricted to firing our rifles in late autumn, winter, and early spring because of dad's garden. Firing my .22 made me feel more grown up. I did not get the same adrenaline rush again until I fired a M1 on the firing range at Fort Bragg during basic training.

CHAPTER 26

Mike Starr's Dog

I, like most of the children in our neighborhood, grew up with some trauma. It did not come from my parents or neighbors but in seeing my pets and friends' pets die. A number of neighborhood dogs were run over by cars on Church Street, which was also US 29 and a busy highway. The most tragic and traumatic incident was seeing Mike Starr's miniature cocker spaniel, who was running with a group of us, race ahead and into the path of a car coming down the hill on Church Street. The owner of the car stopped but the dog was killed instantly. Mike let out a loud cry and the rest of us stood silently looking on in horror. Mike's father, a postman who worked at night and slept during the day, heard the sound of the squealing breaks and recognized his son's cry. He seemed to appear instantly, picked up the limp body of the black and white dog, and tried to comfort his son who could not be consoled.

I find myself still tearful remembering that time. We all went home with heavy hearts. Mike never had another dog and none of us who witnessed what happened ever got over the horror of what we saw.

CHAPTER 27

Oh, Annette!
Favorite Television Shows as a Preteen

My favorite television programs as a preteen are similar to some of the types of programs I still enjoy. My top three were Mutual of Omaha's *Wild Kingdom* with Marlin Perkins and *Victory at Sea* starring the United States military, particularly the Navy, in World War II. I liked *Wild Kingdom* because I loved animals and the show introduced me to many species in a factual and engaging way. *Victory at Sea* had great theme music, a sequential narrative, and action-packed film footage from the Second World War. I was impressed with American bravery in the face of the Japanese and Germans. Our troops were highly skilled, brave, and motivated to serve their country. Mentally, I rooted for them in every episode. Go GIs!

However, as much as I delighted in these two series, my favorite television program came on at 5 p.m. every weekday. It was Walt Disney's *Mickey Mouse Club*! While I was keen on the variety in the show that was not what I appreciated most. No! I was in love with Annette Funicello. She was the epitome of femininity in my 11-year-old mind. I understood immediately that she was the archetype of what a girl should be. I am sure that is why she was the most popular of the original Mouseketeers.

In the mid-1950s, Annette represented a subdued sexiness, the opposite of Marilyn Monroe. I, like a few million other preteen boys, envisioned her as the perfect girlfriend. Her beauty and charm were breathtaking to those of us on the edge of puberty. I would gladly have given up exotic animals and the US Navy for just a few minutes in her presence.

CHAPTER 28

If I Had Been Texas,
Dr. Toomey Would Have Struck Oil

One of the most unpleasant and physically hurting times of my childhood was going to see Dr. Toomey, our dentist, who worked in a house several blocks up Church Street. "Ouch" and "terrified" are the best words that describe my relationship with this dentist. He seemed quite old and had white hair. Even his equipment looked ancient and worn out. It was yellowing. In his waiting room, there were pictures of him and others in World War II. I particularly remember a picture of him with a group of soldiers standing in front of the Taj Mahal.

Every time I went to see Dr. Toomey, it was painful because I had cavities. There was no fluorinated water to help prevent decay. His message to me when he was drilling in my mouth was "Open wide, Sammy." I had changed my name from Sammy to Sam when I was five years old but Dr. Toomey failed to get the message. His instructions for me after every visit were "Don't eat anything for three hours."

Dr. Toomey either died or gave up his practice about the time I was midway through high school. I did not go to him after 10th grade which was about the time I started to wear braces. I am sure underneath his pain-inflicting exterior; he was probably a nice, easy-going individual. Had he been an oilman though, he certainly would have been rich from drilling!

CHAPTER 29

A Homemade Bow and Arrows

COMING TO A POINT

At age 10, I made a bow out of a bent branch I found in the woods below Clairemont School. I put a slit in each end of the stick. Next, I put a string through the slits and made it taut. Afterwards, I found straight sticks I made into arrows to go with the bow, being sure the front of the arrows were sharp. I even split feathers with my pocketknife and pasted or taped them on the back of the arrows. They initially stuck but were flimsy and usually fell off after being shot once or twice. The arrows and the bow were not works of art but they were functional and I took some pride in making them.

On my 12th birthday, my parents bought me a 40-pound fiberglass bow. It was slim, modern and quite a contrast to my primitive bow! They also gave me six regular arrows. I kept the new bow and arrows into my 60s. I loved the bow and the fact that my parents trusted me to use it correctly. It was a point of pride and pleasure.

CHAPTER 30

Transition of Tradition

COINS FROM THE PAST

When I was 11 years old, Pal called me into her room one day. She had something to give me. It was her coin collection. The coins were in a candy tin from the early part of the twentieth century. I especially remember the 1847 penny which was as large as a quarter and the silver dollar bent in a U shape. The latter was taken from a man who had been run over by a train. I think Pal's husband must have preached the dead man's funeral. Other coins I found especially interesting were a Stone Mountain commemorative half dollar from 1925 and a Columbian Exposition half dollar from the Chicago World's Fair of 1893. I especially loved the Indian Head pennies of the late 1800s and early 1900s.

I did not know what to say in appreciation. I know she knew I was grateful and I think she knew I would take care of the coins. Sixty-two years later, I finally parted with most of the coins, selling them, and investing the proceeds into a savings bond for our first grandson, Leo. I thought Pal's investment in me should continue into the next generation, especially since Pal's married name was "Templeman"—the same as Leo's and my middle name.

The gift of the coins is still the one I cherish most from my formative years. I was blessed with a grandparent who was extremely generous even when she had little. I have tried to uphold that spirit in my life as an adult. The gift of the coins was a lesson in giving and its memory has influenced me since. I hope paying it forward in the form of a bond will keep the gift giving.

CHAPTER 31

Perpetuating the Lost Cause

ESSAYS ON CONFEDERATES

The American Civil War had been over physically for almost 100 years when I entered the 5th grade. However, it was not over mentally in the minds of some Southerners, even those in education. My fifth grade teacher and later my sixth grade teacher had our class participate in the Daughters of the Confederacy essay contest and write about famous Confederates. The first year, the essay was on Georgia's Alexander H. Stevens, the Vice President of the Confederacy. The second year we wrote about Nathan Bedford Forrest, a Confederate general and the first Grand Wizard of the Ku Klux Klan. Instead of looking these figures up in the library, we were given pamphlets that contained biographical information on each. The handouts were complimentary in multiple ways.

The essay experience is one that promoted the Lost Cause myth pervasive in the South in the 20th century. The myth focused on the heroic men who fought for or served the Confederacy. My take on what I was being taught was that Southerners were good and virtuous while "Yankees"—God bless you if you said that word—were rude, crude, and evil.

I look back on the Confederate essay days with disbelief that they ever happened. If the goal had been to shape young minds prejudicially, the activity would have been helpful. I am glad I was uncomfortable with the process.

CHAPTER 32

Men in the Hoods

THE KLAN PARADE UP CHURCH STREET

One summer afternoon when I was 10, the Ku Klux Klan cara-vanned into the City of Decatur, which then, as now, is known as a "city of homes, schools, and places of worship." The Klan's participants were mostly from surrounding counties and while the city had issued them a permit for a rally on the courthouse square, they were not exactly welcomed. No one presented them the keys to the city.

The caravan entry route was U.S. 29, Church Street, where we lived. We had a screened in front porch and from there I watched their procession of trucks and cars. It was interesting to note that regardless of the make or model of their vehicles, most had Confederate battle flags—the stars and bars—protruding from their windows or attached to their cars in other ways. A few members of the caravan had on white robes. One had on a hood. They were the men, and women from their self-described invisible empire. To me they were entirely visible.

The Klan parade by our house lasted only a few minutes. Yet, the picture of that time still plays in my mind. The Civil War was not over for them. The hate, discrimination, and misinformation the group spread was like poison sumac. I knew this was not a group to hang with but I would only learn later about most of their infamous deeds. On that hot July day, I was as silent as light and still as a statue. I simply watched.

CHAPTER 33

Cheep, the Fledgling Cardinal

A mong the creatures that made their way into our house was a fledgling Cardinal that had fallen out of its nest. My family nursed it and kept it in our kitchen when it began to try its wings. One day my brother and I were charged with washing the dishes. Russell filled up the sink with hot water and detergent. As he washed, I rinsed and dried. However, in the middle of our job, we decided to go watch a cartoon on television. When we came back, we could not find Cheep who had been flying around the kitchen before we left. Mystified, we decided to finish the dishes and look again. To our shock, we found her body in the dishwater. Cheep must have flown down, thought the white suds on top of the water were solid, and found out too late they were not.

We cried, found a shoebox, and buried Cheep in the garden. I have never liked old cartoons from the 1940s since.

SAMUEL TEMPLEMAN GLADDING

45

CHAPTER 34

The Courthouse and the Blind Man

The courthouse square and the county courthouse that stood in the center of it were main fixtures in the City of Decatur Georgia, when I was growing up. During the weeks of summer, the doors were always open to funnel whatever breeze there was through the lower part of the building. Air conditioning was not common in the South during the 1950s.

I found myself going through the first floor of the courthouse somewhat frequently as a shortcut on my way to see friends or run errands. What stood out to me was a blind man behind a counter selling confections. I wondered how he knew what candy bars people were buying and how to give them change for bills they handed him. How did he distinguish between a Coca-Cola and an Orange Crush? He must have had a system but it was a mystery to me.

I do not know that I needed to be so concerned. He always seemed to be okay. Nevertheless, I worried about him and secretly admired his abilities. I could see what was in my environment. He had to trust those he encountered and feel his way around. In a place where police and criminals mingled, he was an anomaly. I knew justice was supposed to be blind but I did not think the concept extended to those selling candy.

CHAPTER 35

Raising Cotton Instead of Cane

My father loved the soil and enjoyed growing a garden every year. I was not into dirt or vegetables, especially eggplant! However, I was curious. I wanted to see how cotton grew since it was a plant the South had been dependent on for years and was still grown in Georgia. My dad gave me a small plot of land in his garden next to where the Morning Glories and their radiant purple flowers nested on the fence. I hoed the ground and went to a garden shop in downtown Decatur where I bought cottonseed. Returning home, I planted about a dozen seed and waited for Mother Nature and the sun to take over. They did. In a few months, the plants from which the seed sprang had matured. All that was left for me to do was pick the bolls.

To my surprise, the cotton bolls were prickly. They could cut you! Picking cotton was less than romantic. Another discovery I made was how many seed were in bolls. I reaped more seeds than I sowed. I also realized what the phrase "in high cotton" meant. Even at 4 feet 7 inches, my 6th grade height, I had to bend down to pick the cotton. I could just imagine how back breaking picking cotton might be for taller individuals.

I did a show-and-tell report on cotton in my class at school where I shared my stalks and bolls with fellow students and my teacher. The information I presented was rather mundane. Maybe I should have raised cane!

CHAPTER 36

The Horse Stable and the Rock beneath the Ivy

One Sunday afternoon when I was 10, my brother Russell and I went over to play at Carl Jones' house. Carl was Russell's age, a year older than I was. He was smart, outgoing, and funny. Behind Carl's house were woods with a growth of trees that was 20 or 30 years old. Deep within them was a horse stable. It was old but sturdy and must have been used in a bygone era before the trees surrounded and hid it from passersby.

On that particular Sunday, other boys joined us and we formed a "club." One of the initiation rites for being in the club was to jump off the roof of the stable. The older boys did it first and were fine. When my time came, I jumped into the ivy below as the others had. Little did I know there was a rock underneath where I was about to land. Ouch! The rock and my right elbow collided. A sharp pain followed and in getting to my feet, I found not only did my elbow hurt but I could not tighten the muscles in my right arm.

Carl's father was a physician, an allergy specialist. He looked at my elbow and prescribed aspirin. He also said I should keep my right arm in a sling until it felt better. Later, my mother took me to see Dr. Kite, the orthopedist, who had previously worked on my hips. The x-rays he took did not indicate a break he could detect. Hence, I took more aspirin and kept my arm in a sling for several more weeks. The elbow bulged out and I was never able to gain full rotation in the arm again although my muscle tone came back.

The good that came from the stable experience was that years later when I played competitive tennis, I had a much better backhand than forehand because of the angle at which the elbow healed. I also learned to eat with my left hand and to do other activities as a southpaw. In addition, I have an aversion to right wing groups. "Right on!"

CHAPTER 37

The Soap Box Derby
and the Peach Box

One of the most popular events of my childhood was the Soap Box Derby. It was one of the few non-adult sporting events that was shown on television. Rodney Jones, in my 6th grade class, actually built a Soap Box Derby car and later raced it. I thought what he did was "neat" and tried to do something similar, taking four training wheels discarded from our bicycles and attaching them to a large peach box I found in the basement. I had limited success.

I could fit in the peach box but I did not have a steering wheel, any mobility, or brakes. The box would go downhill in a straight line as long as it did not hit a major crack on the sidewalk. After that, all bets on your life were off. I gave up after one run. That is a main reason I am alive today.

CHAPTER 38

My Brother Was a Home Run; I was Strike 3

ittle League was democratic and extremely widespread when I was growing up. It seemed everyone played. All you needed was a glove and athletic skill. While I had the first, I lacked the second. My brother had both. He was an All Star baseball player. He always made the Little League major league teams and was chosen for the All Star teams after the season ended. I can still see him in his Cleveland Indians uniform, which had red pinstripes and the word "Indians" written across the chest in red. Our Uncle Frank took pictures of him that looked professional. As they might say in *Game of Thrones*, he was "a handsome dragon" . . . and a darn good player!

My adventures into Little League did not pay off nearly as well. I seemed to sprain the fingers on my glove hand every year. Ouch! In addition, I flinched when the ball was pitched over the plate. Instead of batting .500, I batted .050! I was terrible! The coaches did not have any problem cutting me from the tryout rosters. I accepted my fate as a Little League failure better than most. I was aware of my skills—or lack thereof. Still, it did not feel good coming home from the tryout field through the shortcut, which was the cemetery behind our house, with sprained fingers, to tell my parents I had yet again not been picked to join a team, especially since Russell Jr. was so good.

Finally, when I was 12, I made a team in what was known as the International Baseball League, an experiment by Little League officials for boys in their last year of eligibility. The powers that were did not want those of us who were older with little or no skill playing baseball to feel like we had little or no skill. It was a nice gesture. Teams had an international name but few of us could pronounce them so we came up with unofficial team names. My teams was known by the players as the "Jabberwocky Blue Jays" and we competed with teams other kids described as the "Awesome Aardvarks," "Crafty Coyotes," "Slimy Salamanders" and "Dirty Dirt Socks." We played on less than an ideal field with red dirt and rocks, behind a dry cleaner building, a few miles from the pristine, finely groomed official Little League facility in Glenlake Park. There was no seating. Everyone stood for as long as they could stand to watch.

As I have indicated, I made the international team because it was my last year of being eligible for Little League. My only dramatic moment was sliding into third base. Other than that, I struck out a lot and made numerous errors in the outfield. After seeing me in one game, my parents never attended another. I did not blame them. There were no awards handed out at the end of a very short season because I do not think anyone wanted to remember what happened with us that summer. It was a relief to stop.

While my failure to become a good baseball player might have been crushing if I had had more ability, to me the constant ceremonial act of not making a Little League team became merely a note in the book of life. Besides, I learned that I could keep the scoreboard in center field over at the Little League field for the major league teams and be rewarded with a moon pie and a RC Cola after the game. Nothing could have been better!

CHAPTER 39

Bucky

ucky was one of the best people I ever knew . . . up to 10th grade. (I am not using Bucky's last name out of respect for his family). Bucky lived on Lucerne Avenue, a modest but nice neighborhood in Decatur. He had an older sister who had been a beauty queen. His mother was welcoming and was a wizard at making the best peanut butter and jelly sandwiches I have ever tasted. I think she put butter on the bread before she put on the spread. Bucky was quick witted and had a personality bigger than the State of Georgia. During the summer between our 6th and 7th grades, I spent the mornings over at Bucky's house before going to deliver my paper route. We worked on Boy Scout projects together and at other times, just had fun watching the model trains in his bedroom circle the tracks. We even formed a band—Lucky and the Misfortunes. Bucky was Lucky. Our band wrote lyrics but did not perform. It was short lived and an education in group dynamics.

In the 7th grade, Bucky and I were both captains of the Safety Patrol during different quarters. The group of teachers who picked the Safety Patrol student to win a free train trip to Washington, D.C. and New York for the national safety patrol parade could not decide between the two of us. Therefore, the principal of the school came in, announced the deadlock, and asked each of us to pick a number between 1 and 10. The boy who was closest to the number on a sheet of paper she held behind her back would win the trip. Bucky went first. He chose 5. With some hesitation, I chose 6. The number was 9. I was overjoyed. I knew my parents could not afford the trip. Yet, I felt sorry for Bucky.

In the 8th grade, Bucky continued to excel. He became our class president as well as a student council representative. His popularity seemed to be boundless. However, in 9th grade, he faded a bit. I think it was because he was working on having fun rather than studying. By 10ᵗʰ grade, he was hanging with the "hoods." I never saw him except behind the stadium bleachers with a group of guys with turned up collars and cigarettes.

Bucky graduated with our class but seemed to disappear after that as if an alien space ship had come and taken him away. I did not know what happened to him until about 10 years later when I found out he had opened an antique store in Underground Atlanta. Apparently, he dealt as much in other substances as he did in antiques. In my 30s, I heard he was in the Atlanta Penitentiary. Tragically, he was in and out of the prison the rest of his life.

In 2016, Bucky died at his son's house south of Atlanta. His obituary did not mention any details of his life. When I read it, all I could think about was how such a promising life ended so terribly. A lesson of age is that good beginnings do not guarantee positive endings and great endings may come when beginnings are rough. Life holds no guarantees.

CHAPTER 40

Joining the
"Goodbye Forever Appendix Club"

Few children think they are going to have appendicitis, let alone one at age 11. I certainly did not. In elementary school, I hardly knew what an appendix was! However, one fall day when I was in 6th grade I discovered my appendix and how much it hurts to remove it.

The day began as usual. I got up and went to school. Afterwards, I came home and had a snack of dark licorice. Just as I was about to go across the street and play in the woods, I realized I did not feel good. Too much licorice? My stomach hurt! As the afternoon wore on, I felt worse. It was a Wednesday and I tried to eat dinner but only took a few bites before retreating to my bed and later throwing up. My parents went to church and when they came home, they brought with them Dr. Jones, our family physician. He pressed down on my abdomen. It smarted! The next thing I knew I was in the car with my parents heading to Georgia Baptist Hospital. They tried to be calm but I sensed they were nervous.

Upon arrival, I was whisked into an operating room and immediately had an appendectomy. Before going under, I threw up again. Being mindful of my manners, I apologized. The medical personnel assured me it was fine and it happened all the time. When I woke up, I was in a children's ward with a lot of pain. I could have sworn the medical team used a hacksaw to remove my former appendage. My agony increased as the anesthesia wore off. If misery loves company, I had a lot of it. In my ward were seven other boys screaming and groaning. It was a cacophony of agonizing moans. If I could have wished, I would have preferred to be in a group of stoic poets. However, it was not to be.

After a week, I was better and allowed to escape the sound, go home, and return to school. The only good moment of my time at Georgia Baptist was when Dr. Hall, our minister, came and after praying over me, gave me a half a dollar! Wow! I was rich in the midst of misery!

I joined my parents the night of my operation in being able to say afterwards "I don't have an appendix" should someone ask, which no one ever did. The process was not one I would ever want to go through again—not even for all the chocolate in Hershey, Pennsylvania. I am thankful that I had but one appendix to give for my health. Losing it left a physical scar but not one anybody could see. If I had been given a choice, I would not have joined the "goodbye forever appendix club." However, I did not have a choice. Physically and psychologically, I was branded forever with a mark signifying the removal. Though the experience is now a memory, I still quiver just a bit when I see dark licorice.

CHAPTER 41

Fort McHenry

A PIANO BOX SAGA

In the 5th grade, I built a "fort" with my friend, Barry Brewton, in the woods on the downward slope of a hill between Clairemont School and Church Street. The interior of our fort was a large cardboard box, in which a piano had been shipped. After getting permission to remove the box from the back of a furniture store in downtown Decatur, we pushed it for about half a mile along the sidewalk to a driveway that ended where the woods surrounding the backside of Clairemont School began. I am sure we had at least another half a mile more of pushing through the trees and brush to our final destination before we reached a spot below the playground of the school that was ideally suited for our structure. Forcing the box forward through the thickets was harder than pushing it on the sidewalk. The terrain was uneven: rugged and steep with stumps, briars, and roots in our way. Yet, we made it. Upon our arrival, we were tired, sweaty, relieved, and happy.

With the box in place, we covered the outside with branches. Our fort appeared to be made of wood! We named the structure Fort McHenry, after Eileen McHenry who was smart, pretty, and personable. Unfortunately, the fort did not last long. In addition to our using it, other kids played in it and rains that came all too soon collapsed the roof of our creation. The demise of Fort McHenry was disappointing but we had a good time while it lasted. Soon we got interested in other activities, Eileen McHenry moved away, and the fort surrendered completely to the elements.

CHAPTER 42

Water works!

A RUSH DOWNSTREAM TO THE RESERVOIR

On a car ride to Richmond, my sister taught me the words to the song "Once there were three fishermen." The song was, and still is, playful with repeating words, such as "fisher, fisher, men, men, men." In the song, the fishermen go to Amsterdam and instead of repeating lyrics per se as a refrain, the song deviates with the words "Amster, Amster, shh, shh, shh" instead of "Amster, Amster, dam, dam, dam." I loved the ending of the song for as a preteen I was forbidden to swear and so instead of singing "shh, shh, shh," I sang "dam, dam, dam," and my words were not considered profane.

Outside of the song, I was like many preteen boys and enjoyed building dams better than singing about them. One summer day, a group of us built a dam on Glen Creek across the street from Glenlake Swimming Pool. During the middle of our construction, it started getting cloudy and before we knew it, a rather heavy rain started to fall. Inspired by the rain, we worked harder to build our dam and back the water up. We were successful and decided we should strategically break the dam when the water got to a certain level. The idea was we could ride the water to the city reservoir at the edge of town several miles away. We had enough inner tubes with us so each boy had one. When we broke the dam, we were all swept away. However, as in-the-moment 12 year olds we had not counted on the drainage pipes that went under the streets on our route. When navigating through them we were underwater and had to take a deep breathe before entering and hope for the best.

The Good Lord looks after fools, and in our case, young adolescent boys. All five of us made it to the reservoir and celebrated what we had accomplished. It had been thrilling as well as a little scary. Tired, but joyful, we walked the several miles back home carrying our inner tubes. In the back of our minds we were glad we had survived. We also wished we could do it again, but this time without going through the drainage pipes!

CHAPTER 43

Touchdown!
The Miracle of the Miscues

The Big Three sports of the 1950s were football, basketball, and baseball. While baseball was king, the YMCA sponsored elementary school programs in football and basketball. For football, you needed a helmet and shoulder pads. For basketball, all you needed was a jersey and shorts. Most boys, regardless of ability, played in the Y programs. A league was set up between the elementary schools in the City of Decatur School System and on Saturday mornings, games were played. There was one practice each week. The coach for Clairemont School was John Moler, a somewhat rotund divinity student at nearby Emory University. John had a brother, Paul, who was in my grade and one of the few who did not play sports. It was understandable. His right arm had withered away a few years earlier when he had polio. Paul wore that arm in a sling. He could play baseball well one handed but football and basketball were out of the question.

I was not big, fast, coordinated, or strong but John Moler put me in to play defensive end every now and then. I simply had to grab the flag of the boy who was running the ball. One time, we played a championship game where the quarterback was purported to weigh 125 pounds! As a 65-pound hunk of protoplasm, I was intimidated. However, most football Saturdays I rushed in a few yards and waited for a boy with the football to run my way. The best Saturday of my Y football career came when a boy who was carrying the ball fumbled near me. In the mayhem that followed, the ball rolled backwards. In the chaos, I stumbled and fell on it. The referee unsure of who I was playing for asked me. I said "Clairemont." He then raised his hands over his head and signaled "Touchdown." I was thrilled!

Years later, I compared what happened to a blind squirrel finding nuts. It was the miracle of the miscues. Unlike the blind squirrel, there was no skill involved in my scoring a touchdown. After the game, I ran home. Only Pal was home sitting over one of the floor radiators getting warm. I told her the good news and shared it with the rest of the family later. No one was as excited as I was. It was an accidental moment that elevated my ego, gave me sweet dreams, and eventually led to my further understanding of athletics. It also provided me insight into the nature of luck.

CHAPTER 44

Dr. Kite, Moses, and the Fruit Cakes

D
r. Hiram Kite, as mentioned earlier, was the orthopedic surgeon who operated on my brother and me when we had dislocated hips. He was a kind and competent man who was a national
authority on hips. He made it possible for my brother and me to walk
and run.

Up through the 7th grade, my brother and I had annual checkups
with him at Scottish Rite Hospital. While I liked Dr. Kite, I hated the
checkups. The hospital gowns were open in the back. In addition, you
had to wear white loincloths instead of your underwear. In the early
days, I remember my mother singing a song to us as we changed.
It went:

> Feel so fine; feel so good, headed to the rock where Moses stood,
> Where I put on my long white robe.
> Sing "Halla, Halla . . . lu . . . jah, Sing Halla, Halla . . . lu . . . jah"

In appreciation for Dr. Kite's skills, every year my mother would
make a fruitcake that my brother, Russell, and I, along with my father
would take to him at Christmas. Dr. Kite was always grateful and gra-
cious but never could remember our names. He always called one of
us "David." We continued the tradition even after I went to college. It
was an important way of saying "Thank you." Getting our names right
did not matter. We knew his and what he had done.

CHAPTER 45

Chum

Walter Chrietzberg was one of my best friends in the 5th grade. I think my first sleepover was actually at Walter's. Regardless, his family owned a farm where they would occasionally go. After one summer weekend, I received a call from Walter. After hello came a question: "Would you like a puppy?" Walter explained a car had driven up and unloaded five puppies in a field on his family's farm. He still had two to give away. My dad was at work so I asked my mom and she took me over to see them. I found one of the two pups was quite people oriented. Mom said I could take the puppy home and I could then speak to dad about the matter when he came home.

I played some baseball that afternoon and when I arrived back home, with sprained fingers of course, my father was already in his garden. My next move was instinctive. I picked up the puppy and went out the back door to the garden where my father was weeding. I explained to him the story of how I got the puppy and that I could return it. His version of the story, which I later found he told his friends, was sentimental. However, all I remember him saying at the time was "yes." He had had a dog named "Jack" as a boy and my mother had had a collie as a girl.

I named my new canine "Chum" because he was to be my friend. Chum, as a Heinz 57—a mixture of many breeds—was relegated to being an outdoor dog. He slept on rags and bags inside the basement door. He was sometimes a bit wild but he learned to sit and shake before every meal. Pal, who fed him once, said he would not touch his food until he had shaken her hand. She wondered if she was going to have to say grace with him after that. She did not.

Just before we moved from Church Street at the end of my senior year in high school, Chum started digging and trying to get out of the fence. Once when he did, he ended up at our vet's about a mile away. When we moved to Lamont Drive that summer, Chum dug under our fence there and made his way back to Church Street on several occasions. After I went off to college, Chum continued to dig and get out. My parents and sister were all working and my brother was a sophomore in college playing baseball and in a fraternity. In other words, everyone was busy and Chum had ample opportunities to slip under the fence. I know everyone looked for him but by Thanksgiving, he had completely disappeared. We never found him.

My brother once romanticized what happened. He envisioned Chum digging out and continuing to exercise his freedom to roam around Decatur. He thought we might all be reconnected some day in Heaven. Although I doubt that will happen, I am grateful for having had Chum for as long as we did. It was wonderful growing up with him!

CHAPTER 46

First Kiss

PERMISSION BUT NO PASSION

My first, and only kiss, before high school was with Nancy Honea at a 6th grade party at Ann Graham's house on Clairemont Avenue. I was infatuated with Nancy. She was no Annette Funicello of Disney fame, but at age 11, she was as close to Annette as I was going to get. My time of romancing Nancy was rather brief lasting less than a year. She went to the First Baptist Church and was in the choir and Sunday School with me as well as in my elementary school class. She also lived across the street from Walter Chrietzberg, one of my closest friends, with whom I occasionally spent the night.

I remember thinking as a sixth grader that it was time I kissed a girl. Nancy must have thought something similar but substituted the word "boy" for "girl." I asked permission before leaning over to kiss her. The kiss was exactly that, a kiss. There was no follow-up, no second kiss. There were no lipstick smears and little tingling up and down the spine. That was fine. We had both gained experience with the opposite sex. It was all we had sought and all we got.

CHAPTER 47

Railroad Placards and Model Cars

Cereals that appealed to children in the 1950s promoted themselves through giving away items children liked. I am sure my parents were chagrined and felt trapped by this practice just as parents do today. One of the cereals my brother and I liked gave away metal railroad placards. I was particularly drawn to the Union Pacific railroad sign as well as the one that read "New Haven"—a place where I would later live for two years. The placards were fun to collect and we could stick them on wagons, bikes, and doors.

More interesting than the railroad placards were plastic model cars that we bought at the Hobby Shop. The outside of the boxes were deceptive in showing the models that had been glued together. The task of assembling the pieces was much harder than it looked although the salespeople at the Hobby Shop did not tell us. First, the plastic parts had to be separated from each other. Next, we had to follow the instructions, which were sometimes painstakingly complex. Nevertheless, with patience and the help of a strong glue, we assembled the cars. The work was not finished until we painted our models. Little bottles of paint and fine tipped paintbrushes made the job tedious but fun. We even bought a wooden rack to display up to six of our cars. My favorite was the Stanley Steamer. As a 5th grader, I did not understand how it failed to become the most popular car in America. Of course, I did not understand in the 8th grade why the Edsel failed either.

Putting the plastic model cars together taught my siblings and me patience and helped us develop pride in our work. The railroad placards helped us cultivate a knowledge of the United States and a sense of adventure. Outcomes of our efforts were both obvious and discrete.

CHAPTER 48

Paper Route

A CAREER ENLIGHTENING EXPERIENCE

When my brother and I were 11 and 10 respectively, my father wanted us to have a paper route. I think he was trying to teach us the importance of hard work and that through such a process a person could earn money and build character. Regardless, my brother got a route when he was in the sixth grade and I was in the fifth. The route was on Church Street where we lived. It started at the Candler Hotel. They took 10 papers. It ended at the house before Glenlake Park.

Russell and I split the route. I had 25 papers to deliver starting just past the entrance to the Decatur City Cemetery. The route was downhill and I could deliver it quickly in about 30 to 35 minutes. However, I had to set aside about two hours a day for delivering the papers. It took time to get to the paper route office, time to unload the newspaper truck, time to count out the papers for the route, and time to peddle a one-speed bike with newspapers in the front basket to the route. In the summer, I went to get the papers around 2 or 2:30 p.m. During the school year, I went to pick up the papers right after school.

In the 6th grade, I got my own route—65 papers in the Great Lakes area of Decatur where all the streets were named for Great Lakes. The process of delivery took longer since I now had 40 more papers than before. Thursdays were hard because of advertisement sections that had to be inserted into the papers by hand. Sundays were twice as difficult as Thursdays because the paper was thicker and the inserts were too. Our father helped my brother and me on Sundays getting us up around 5 a.m. and driving us to our routes with the car loaded down full of papers. We threw the combined edition of the *Atlanta Journal and Atlanta Constitution* with its motto "Covers Dixie like the Dew." When we had finished my dad would sometimes stop and then run the red light at the corner of Geneva and Church Streets. It was a kind of celebration ceremony for having finished. It was also the only time I believe my father ever broke the law.

The worst thing about having the paper route was collecting on Saturday morning, especially from the people who paid weekly and those who never seemed to have any money. Then there were customers who swore you were collecting twice and would not pay you, or who moved away without telling or paying you. I never liked collecting. It took time, patience and diplomacy. I had one older couple who thought I was there to visit them and talked my ears off. I learned never to go inside their house. Most customers were nice but it still took time and effort.

In the summers, I would have enjoyed going to the swimming pool at Glenlake rather than to the paper office. During the school year on Wednesdays, it was usually off to church for choir soon after I finished my route. Choir was an activity I was not fond of because my voice was changing and our director was artsy and condescending. After choir, it was home for supper, then off to church again for Royal Ambassadors, a boys' group that involved memorizing lots of scripture, and afterwards for Prayer Meeting which I prayed would be finished in less than an hour. It never was. On good nights at 9:30 p.m. our family arrived back home and I started my homework. I remember telling my 6th grade teacher one Thursday morning I had been up past midnight working on my assignments. After that, she eased off homework on Wednesday nights and my delighted classmates called me "Saint Sam." Still, it was unusual for me to finish my homework until quite late on Wednesdays.

I gave up the paper route right as I entered 8th grade. It was nice to let it go—a major relief! My mother had returned to teaching 4th grade by then and my father was making a decent salary running his own business. I have many memories from throwing papers. The most dramatic was when my bike turned over in a Thursday thunderstorm and I had to throw myself on top of the papers to keep them dry. My mother must have sensed something was wrong and found me on the courthouse square on top of the papers. With an umbrella over her head, she helped me get the papers into the car and none were ruined.

I did not make a lot of money as a paperboy. What money I made my parents insisted I save at the DeKalb Credit Union where the manager's first name was "Wheat." I will always wonder how Wheat's parents could name him that. Maybe they were from Kansas and thought the name quite masculine. However, if they were going for a grain name "Barley" would have been more masculine.

Through the process of having a paper route I realized I did not want to earn a living doing manual labor, getting up before sunrise to go to work, or being in business collecting money to make a living. I think I could have made these career decisions without having thrown papers but they were affirmed by my experience.

CHAPTER 49

Sex at Church

THE ABCS OF PHYSIOLOGY

When I was first told there was going to be sex at church, I did a double take. The Baptists I knew were against dancing and hay rides, how could they be for sex, especially in the church? I was 12 years old—a tween. I had no idea initially what was about to occur was sex education. I am still amazed it occurred on Sunday nights in Training Union. A couple of doctors led it.

The education was all about the physical side of sex, after all we were being led by physicians. Boys and girls were broken up into two distinct groups and the lessons were specific to each sex. I learned more about the opposite sex in two weeks than most of my friends learned in 18 years. If I had been given an anatomical doll of a girl after the class, I could have named every part and recited what happened when and how. Of course, any of the psychological and emotional parts of a union were left out except for the mantra "you only have sex with someone you love."

I am glad I missed "the Talk" my dad would have given me about sex. Since my father was raised on a farm, "the Talk" would probably have been illustrated with examples of cows, chickens, and horses. The results might have left me more confused than before except for the fact I would have known more about calves, chicks, and colts.

CHAPTER 50

Rockets

A POSITIVE WAY OF SPACING OUT

In the 7th grade, I fell in love with aerospace, particularly rockets. I remember saving paper towel rolls and paper machining them in the shape of a rocket complete with a "nose" on top. I put saltpeter, which I bought from the drug store pharmacy, mixing it with charcoal in the tubes. I then papier-mâchéd over the bottom except for a small hole where I inserted a fuse. When the papier-mâché dried, I took my rockets to the playground at Clairemont School and tried to launch them.

My attempts at getting a rocket in the air were usually total failures resulting in some swift burning fires from the bottom of the rocket on up. However, I did win an honorable mention in the 8th grade science fair for one of my rockets. Some of the men who worked for my father helped me solder some metal together into the shape of a rocket. I tried to launch it after the fair but alas, I did not get a liftoff. Getting into space, other than mentally when I spaced out, was harder than I thought.

CHAPTER 51

Richmond and Mr. Rutland

THE MOVE THAT DID NOT MOVE US

At the end of my sixth grade year, my parents gathered us together for a family meeting. Sometimes we had daily Bible readings and discussions but I could tell immediately that this was not such an occasion. My parents looked serious and within a few minutes, I knew why. My father announced his company was transferring him to Richmond, Virginia. My heart sank. I did not want to leave Decatur. I had good friends and genuinely liked the city. My siblings were not as reluctant to leave and I did not understand why. Maybe they were more adventuresome.

We did not end up in Richmond because of a number of circumstances. For one, the people at my father's company would not tell him what his job would be. Their vagueness made my dad reluctant. About the same time, Guy W. Rutland, who served on the Board of Deacons with my father at Decatur First Baptist, offered to set him up as the manager and eventually owner of one of his businesses. Mr. Rutland realized my father had talent even though he did not have a college degree.

My dad now had choices. He knew what the future was if he stayed in Decatur. As the summer matured so did my father's resolve not to move. At age 48, he started over leaving behind 27 years of work with V-C Chemical Company. It was a smart decision. Our family's socioeconomic status improved considerably. I could not have been more pleased. I loved Decatur!

CHAPTER 52

The Dark Room of Enlightenment

At age 12, I became interested in photography. I asked for a photography development kit for my birthday and I received one. The kit was not extensive but it had instructions and the chemicals needed for processing film. Before trying to develop my pictures, I checked with my family about whether I could use the bathroom for a dark room. Upon getting permission and making sure everyone's bladder was empty, I proceeded. My negatives came out fine and I was able to print black and white pictures.

Even though my bathroom dark room worked fine, I eventually ran out of chemicals and could not afford more. I also realized my family preferred to use a professional photo shop to develop and print their pictures. Maybe if we had had a second bathroom and I had had money to purchase chemicals I would have taken a different career path from the one I chose. Still, the exposure did me good.

CHAPTER 53

Just as I Am

A CALLING TO AFRICA!

G rowing up Baptist was mentally challenging—at least in my child-hood church where the emphasis was on record keeping, recita-tion, and evangelism. On Sunday School mornings, each child had to fill out a 7-point record form checking such categories as "on time," "read lesson," and "brought Bible." In addition to the records, there was a focus on memorizing scripture most of which was from the New Testament, Psalms, and Proverbs. I was never asked to recite any-thing from the Song of Solomon.

I did fine in the first two categories of being a Baptist—keeping a record of my attendance and memorizing scripture. However, the third emphasis, evangelism, seemed a bit irrelevant to me until one summer day when the weather and our minister both got hot. I was 12 years old and seated with my family in the 11 a.m. worship ser-vice in the fifth pew on the left hand side of the sanctuary—a place our family claimed for years. On that summer Sunday, when the ser-mon ended, the minister gave the traditional invitation for anyone who wished to come forward and join the church as the congregation sang: "Just as I am."

Several verses were sung and no one came. Therefore, the min-ister asked everyone to bow their heads and close their eyes while the choir sang the hymn slowly and with feeling. He said he was sure the Lord was calling someone that day but he was not sure exactly what he or she was being called for. I was sure the Lord did not have my number so I relaxed. However, after the choir had sung and no one had responded, the minister asked the congregation to sing some more. Two, then three, verses were sung of "Just as I am." Still there was no one in the front of the church except the preacher. Maybe the Lord was being active over at the First Presbyterian Church. At least the thought entered my mind.

Somewhat frustrated, out minister asked for the head-bowing, eye-closing response again while the choir sang softly in the background. When his expectations were not met, he said to the congregation's surprise:

"I want everyone who has volunteered to be a missionary to Africa to come to the front."

"Sam" he said, "that's you and Sandra" pointing to one of my friends who was the same age as me.

I was stunned but began to make my way to the aisle past my parents and siblings who seemed a bit shocked that I was being called to Africa. Coming down the aisle towards the front, I saw my friend, Sandra, who was a pretty girl, with long blond hair, blue eyes, and a smile that could melt the heart of almost any preadolescent boy. However, this morning, she was not radiant or smiling and looked upset. To make matters worse, she was crying. The tears ran down her face in small steams eroding her make-up significantly. When I asked why she was so distressed she sobbed out:

"I don't want to go to Africa as a missionary!"

"I'm not too wild about the idea myself" I replied in one of the great understatements of my life.

Nevertheless, we made our way to the front where the pastor had us stand in line and be greeted by anyone who so chose to come by after the service.

Because of the time that had been taken up with the invitation, most people chose to hurry home to what was a traditional large Sunday noonday meal in the South. Only a handful of the faithful came to shake our hands and wish us well as we stood there in disbelief. One of the most ardent of the faithful was at the front of the line. It was "Miss Thelma!" She was an older woman who was in church every time the doors opened. She was a great supporter of foreign missions and shook my hand so vigorously I found my whole body vibrating.

"God bless you child," I remember her saying while thinking, "God is probably the only one who can bless us and I really wish the Almighty would make us invisible right now."

Had the story ended there, I would have been humiliated and humbled but happy. However, this bizarre Sunday event had a life of its own. The rest of my teenage years and into college was influenced by it. As old as I thought Miss Thelma was, she was not ancient enough to stop coming to church and asking me how my preparation to serve in Africa was coming along. Every Sunday during the school year, I would see her and she would quiz me about Africa, such as what was the capital of Liberia, where was the Congo, and whether there were a lot of elephants in Nigeria. Over time I became pretty good in mastering African geography and history. The constant questioning from Miss Thelma stopped only when I went off to college.

At that juncture in my life, Miss Thelma had truly grown old and a bit senile. Nevertheless, she kept coming to church and would inevitably find me whenever I was home for breaks. She assumed by the time I was 18 that I was in Africa and only home on furloughs, which seemed too frequent and regular in her mind. She asked me how my missionary work was going and since I was a Georgian at a North Carolina school, I interpreted her question broadly, telling her that I was doing my best to minister to the heathen who surrounded me daily in "the Forest," i.e., Wake Forest. I assured her the uneducated were being taken care of regularly. She would smile and walk away.

As the years went by, Miss Thelma became frail and too weak to attend church. Sandra got married and moved away, and I eventually changed denominations and became a United Methodist. Although my awareness of others and myself increased a lot from being called forward to the front of my church that fateful Sunday, most of what I learned came later. It specifically manifested itself in the form of being able to think quickly on my feet and to memorize multiple facts about a distant continent. I finally went to South Africa in 2006 but as far as I know Sandra never went any further than Savannah. I doubt either of us will ever be missionaries at this juncture in our lives but I am sure the memory of that Sunday morning will dwell in our minds forever.

The Lord certainly works in mysterious ways. Understanding what happens, when and for what reason is not necessarily something we are privileged to know so I doubt I will ever solve the Africa calling of so many years ago. It does seem to me though that when people are allowed to make their own decisions, they enjoy life better. Not everyone needs to be volunteered for service in Africa. However, everyone needs to learn geography and history. Thanks to Miss Thelma, I did!

Amen!

CHAPTER 54

Cardboard Sliding and Pinecone Battles

It did not snow often in Decatur and so any snow related activities on an extended basis were not possible. Nevertheless, my peers and I tried to compensate. Instead of snowboarding, we went cardboard sliding, an activity that simply required a piece of cardboard big enough for you to sit on and a steep hill. The most fun was when friends pushed you off and your cardboard bobsled would go racing down a hill at breakneck speeds. On your trip down, you could maneuver yourself, using your hand and feet and yell "Geronimo," or "Oh No!" Hopefully, you missed the trees and other hazardous obstacles, such as rocks, that might be on your course.

Another pastime was pinecone fights, similar to snowball fights except they were bloodier. The cones were hard and did not explode into particles of a powdery substance when they hit. Pinecone fights, like snowball fights, consisted of teams. Once a team was chosen, members had a few minutes to gather pinecones. Soon thereafter the fight was on. Each team member tried to hit an opponent with a pinecone or two and drive the enemy from the field. Kids who could find them used trashcan lids to protect themselves from opponents' cones.

I do not remember anyone ever getting seriously hurt from these two non-snow pastimes. A few of my friends did get bloody noses, scrapes and a few bruises. They wore them proudly. In the heat of a pinecone fight though, all I could wish for was snow!

PART III

Adolescence (13–17 Years Old)

In the late 1950s, at least in Decatur, Georgia, a child went from elementary school to high school. There were no middle schools. The jump was from being a 7th grader to being a "subfreshman"—an 8th grader—in high school. As subfreshmen we changed classes but all our classes were on the top floor of the North Building. Upperclassmen were in other parts of the North Building and in the South Building. The cafeteria and gym where food and exercise were offered were in the Central Building where everyone mingled before and after school and during lunch periods. The football field behind the school buildings was for physical education.

Most of us became more sophisticated as we advanced in years and grades. Still, there was a lot of awkwardness. Frustration, braces, acne, and heartaches were part of high school life as were elations, smiles, Clearasil, and embraces. Like adolescents everywhere, we grew to be more like adults with notable regressions on occasions. It was a time of significant and sometimes rapid physical, cognitive, behavioral, and affective change. I both loved and loathed aspects of it.

CHAPTER 55

Dancing in Rebellion

My biggest adolescent rebellion was one none of my friends had. It involved dancing. My mother thought dancing was sinful, an attitude I am sure she acquired as the daughter of a Baptist minister. None of the Gladding children ever took dancing lessons. It was not a topic of discussion. What we learned about dancing we acquired from watching Dick Clark's American Bandstand on television or from imitating friends.

I know it perturbed all the Gladding children but I think it may have affected me most. I was a social animal and was upset that we were not allowed to move our feet to a musical beat in any meaningful and delightful way. It seemed like so much fun and it was a good way to meet girls. Finally, my mother relented but only reluctantly. During the summer of my 8th grade year, I was allowed to go to "The Canteen"—an event held at the Decatur Recreation Center for my age group, where there was a jukebox, dance floor, pool tables, and a soda fountain. I mostly hung around the dance floor and talked with friends, and yes, I danced.

I did not ask my parents to drive me to or from the Recreation Center. I did not want to "stir the waters." Instead, I kept a low profile. I walked the mile or so to the Recreation Center every Saturday night around 7 p.m. and footed it home around 10 p.m. I loved going to the Canteen and did not mind walking back and forth. That 8th grade summer was one of the best times of my life. It gave me confidence as well as some dance steps and friends. Ironically, four years later my parents were asked to chaperone my graduation dance at the end of my senior year in high school. They did . . . and even seemed to have a good time. Dances and people change over time.

CHAPTER 56

Welcome to High School

I looked forward to going to high school. After all, my sister and brother were already there! I knew a little of what to expect and I thought high school students were "cool." Changing classes, a chance to meet new people, going to athletic events and sock hops, what was there not to like? I did not realize balancing home and extra curricular events would be a challenge.

To start the year, there was a welcoming reception for 8th graders one August afternoon. It included a tour of the school. The atmosphere seemed friendly. Bobby Defoor, a senior who went to our church and was an outstanding athlete, was one of the Student Government co-presidents. At the end of the orientation, he along with other student leaders handed out 6-ounce bottles of Coca-Colas. The day was hot. The drink was cold. The atmosphere was warm. As I went to leave, I remember thinking: "I'm going to like it here." . . . and for the most part, I did.

CHAPTER 57

Mapping It Out

A DREAM

I know it will sound nerdy and obsessive compulsive but before I entered high school, I mapped out what I wanted to do. I looked through my sister's yearbooks and targeted activities I thought would be interesting and fulfilling such as student government, ROTC, and playing basketball. However, much of what I did was not planned, such as being a football manager or working on the yearbook, while others like playing basketball never materialized.

I think having an ambition to do something meaningful helped me keep going when I ran into adversity and disappointment. It was that spirit, i.e., determination, rather than my abilities that encouraged and allowed me to move forward. Dreams made me more than I would have otherwise been. Acceptance of newness and failure helped me mature and learn.

CHAPTER 58

Sissy, Really?

M y 9th grade year was rough. After having had a solid 8th grade year, I went down socially. It was like walking on ice; I could not seem to get my footing. The teachers I had were fine but not exciting. I am not sure why I kept slipping.

The deepest valley of a rather low year came when one of the best players on the B Team football squad called me a sissy one day at lunch. He was considered "hot"—a BMOC, a Big Man on Campus—but he was socially inept. Regardless, there I was being called the worst name a 14-year-old could imagine and in front of some classmates. I was almost speechless but not knowing what else to do, I asked my adversary why he had called me such a name. He was not the smartest student ever and I caught him off guard. He was silent. Finally, he said "because you are." I replied "that's not good enough." Tension followed. At 5′ 2″ and 115 pounds, I knew I was outmatched physically, so I simply walked away.

As fate would have it, my nemesis was promoted to the varsity squad his sophomore year and I became a football manager at the same time. It may not seem like a football manager would have any power over a player but managers are the ones who hand out equipment and tape ankles before practices and games. They actually have some influence on players. I decided early on I would not take revenge and I continued that stance through my senior year but I was tempted.

The outstanding B team player never made the starting lineup during his tenure on the varsity. Part of it was because of his poor attitude toward others on the squad. Part of it was because his abilities did not mature. I feel good that I lived up to what my faith would teach me, which was "do good to your enemies." I regret the moment of embarrassment I experienced as a 9th grader. I am glad I chose to walk away from a label and not hold a grudge. It made a positive difference.

CHAPTER 59

Misfits with No Fix

J on and Robin were, at best, misfits during high school. I tried to befriend each but with no success. They were both looking for attention and maybe acceptance but the way they went about attracting others to themselves hurt them—literally. Jon's gimmick was to tout the virtues of Communism. In the 1960s, such a message was anathema. Robin, on the other hand, just acted "crazy" by making funny sounds, telling off colored jokes that were not funny, and generally being a pest. He was constantly being chased, taunted, and beaten up. Both boys went to my church and were in the same youth groups to which I belonged. Their parents were pillars in the church—nice people—but they were unable to control either teen.

Both Jon and Robin died young in their early 20s. I felt deeply about them but was unable to influence either. I wonder if mental health services had been more available, beyond a predominant psychoanalytic approach that dominated the landscape then, if they would have been able to adjust or survive. I wonder also if their bizarre behaviors and the fact they did not receive the treatment they needed may have influenced my going into a mental health profession. My heart still aches when I think of who they were, who they might have become, and what happened to them. Both had potential but neither learned what to do with it. They were American tragedies.

CHAPTER 60

Making the Grades . . . Almost

I thought I had some intelligence as teenager but when compared to the top tier of students at Decatur High School, I was on a secondary level. As Jo Dee Messina's lyrics would later describe, but in another context, I was "above the low but below the upper." I did not have a STEM mind and I was not especially fast in picking up complex concepts. To make matters worse, my spelling and pronunciation of words were abysmal. When I was told to look up words in the dictionary, I often did not succeed because I could not decipher the letter the word began with or certain vowels and consonants. For instance, when the orchestra from the Baptist Children's Home visited our church—and they did so twice—I could have sworn the minister said their orphanage was in "Hateville" not "Hapeville." That seemed very odd and ungodly! There was also the matter of leaving letters out of words or adding them in. For instance, I spelled "library" as "libary" until my first year in college. To rectify this problem, I later married a librarian. Then, there was pronunciation. I usually mispronounced words I had never seen before, even one-syllable words. I also eschewed words that began with certain letters, like "w" because I could not get the sound right.

In order to combat my deficiencies, I developed a routine for studying and completing my homework. It involved rote memorization. After supper, I went to the room in the back of the house, the bedroom where Pal and Peggy slept. It had a desk, lamp, and space for my schoolbooks as well as school notebooks. There, I tackled my homework assignments starting with hardest one first. I was focused and occasionally would finish before my grandmother and sister were ready to come to bed. By bedtime, my head was full of facts.

I cannot say I enjoyed this weekday routine of memorizing, although I liked learning and my ritualistic behavior helped me get better grades than I would have otherwise. I almost made the National Honor Society but was two points shy on my overall grade point average—an 88 as opposed to 90. I did make the Beta Club, which required an average of 85. I was at peace knowing I was doing the best I could but my biggest wish was for a more functional brain.

CHAPTER 61

Boy Scouts and the Badges

Thursday evening from 7 to 9 p.m. was Boy Scout night. I joined Troop 134 along with my brother, Russell. It was sponsored by our church—First Baptist Church of Decatur—while the First Methodist Church supported the super troop of Decatur—175. We met in a Quonset hut near the back of the 12-acre campus of the church. Inside the Quonset hut was a potbelly stove that kept us warm in the winter and where I once received a bad headache and head bruise when I ran into it playing Blind Man's Bluff.

I started my scouting experience in the beginning of the sixth grade after an uneventful stint of two years in Cub Scouts. I enjoyed the weekly meetings especially when we would play games outside like Fox and Hounds. Bucky, my best friend at the time was also in Boy Scouts and we tackled a number of merit badges together and were members of the Flying Eagles patrol. Cooking was the most challenging and we had to do it twice to pass. For two years, I went with the troop to Camp Bert Adams, where I passed swimming, and Camp Altoona, where I failed canoeing. Our other camping trips during the year were fun, too, except when I lost my tennis shoes in the Yellow River and had to go barefoot for a day and a half.

Our troop leaders and the boys in the troop were focused more on fun than achievement. I wanted both. My inner spirit would not let me settle for just having a good time. After all, the man I had been named for, Samuel Templeman, had been given the Silver Beaver for his work with Boy Scouts. Over the months, I mostly played on Thursday nights and earned merit badges on weekends, especially Sundays when the Gladding clan shut down on doing anything fun.

In my sophomore year in high school I realized if I did not earn the last merit badges for my Eagle soon, I was going to become ineligible to get it. Somewhat alone, because my brother and friends had dropped out, I earned the final badges and for good measure earned the God and Country Award. Because of the time it took to process my application, I did not receive my Eagle until the fall of my junior year. It was a countywide court of honor ceremony at the DeKalb Courthouse with only four boys receiving the rank.

As good as it felt to obtain the highest award in Scouting, it was anticlimactic. I was grateful for what had been but the Boy Scouts had taken a backseat in my life since none of my friends were in it anymore. High school academics and extracurricular activities took their time and mine. The result was that I never attended another Scouting event again until my sons joined Boy Scouts. Still, on the fall night when my mother pinned the Eagle Scout Award on me, I was proud and wished Bucky had been as determined.

CHAPTER 62

Looking for Athletic Support

When I was growing up user-friendly, big box, athletic equipment stores were rare. If you needed balls, bats, clubs, gloves or other sporting paraphernalia, you got them at a department store, such as Sears. My first tennis racket, a Poncho Gonzales special, was bought at Rich's, which was the largest department store in Atlanta. Yet, while there were many outlets for basic athletic equipment, buying the supportive gear to go with these items was not always easy.

At age 14, I realized I needed an athletic supporter, informally known as a jockstrap. The only place to buy one in Decatur was at a drug store. However much to my dismay, you could not just go and pick up the support you needed off a shelf because this specialty item was kept in a glass case behind the counter in the pharmacy section. You had to interact with a live person and ask for what you wanted including the make and size. Sometimes there were women salespeople at the counter. Asking them for a jockstrap was something I felt uncomfortable doing even though I had completed "Sex in the Church" and there was nothing "immoral," "lewd," or "embarrassing" about my request.

Given the situation, I "suffered." I did not think my need was one I could bring up in casual conversation with classmates like "Hey, Bob, I need a jockstrap. Got any good ideas of what fits best?" I must have gone to the drug store pharmacy three times before I blurted out what I wanted. In the meantime, I had purchased a bottle of calamine lotion, some acne cream, and cough syrup. When I finally said the words "athletic supporter" the older, balding man who was waiting on me smiled and said to my relief as he pulled a box off the shelf: "This is what I would recommend." He then explained why it would work best, handed me the box, took my money, and put my purchase in a brown nondescript paper bag—the kind that might arouse suspicion as to what was in it had it been an older teen.

I had mixed feelings walking home. I was pleased I had the support I had been seeking but I was perturbed it had taken me so long. The important point is my need had been met. I slept well that night.

CHAPTER 63

Saying "No" to the Skimpy Speedo

S ince I was not big enough to play football or basketball and was a klutz at baseball, I decided to try sports where I had a chance of success. One of my first choices was swimming. My parents had provided my siblings and me with Red Cross swimming lessons when we were growing up, so I felt confident in a pool, especially doing the breaststroke. There were no tryouts for the swim team because there were not many guys who signed up for it. Decatur High did not have a pool and I had no access to a pool, except in summer. Thus, I practiced my strokes on smooth surfaces and in the air. Neither did me much good. Another complicating factor to my career as a swimmer was I did not like the sound of the starter pistol. Nevertheless, I stayed on the team my freshman and sophomore years where at best I was mediocre. My sophomore year, I lettered though because of a fluke. Here is how it happened.

The Georgia High School Boys Championship Swim Meet was being held at Emory University that year. While I was not one of the boys on our medley relay team, one of the guys on the team got sick the morning of the meet. Soon thereafter, I received a call from Dick Pittman the team captain asking if I could swim in the meet. I had not practiced with the team and had little idea of what to do but I agreed. My mother took me over to the Emory pool and there I became a part of the team. I swam the third leg of the relay—50 yards. The good news is I made it. The bad news is our team came in last. Still, we were officially the sixth best relay team in the State of Georgia and we all received ribbons.

A friend of mine, Joe, heard of our triumph since it was in the school paper, *The Scribbler*. Shortly thereafter, when I was at his house, he tried to give me a rather skimpy blue Speedo swimsuit. I was horrified and politely but firmly said "you shouldn't have," which he really should not have, or "I couldn't possibly accept such a terrible gift." Indirectly and directly in the best Southern dialect of the time, I tried to convey I did not want what he was offering without hurting his feelings. Frustrated, I finally make my refusal official by telling Joe I was finishing my swimming career "on top." I knew I would never finish as high as I had on that fateful morning when I substituted in for a sick team member. I hope Joe took the Speedo back to the store. Only the swim gods know if he did.

CHAPTER 64

For the Love of a Game

TENNIS

Tennis was somewhat of an easy sport for me to master. The reason was my backhand was surprisingly good because of my misshaped elbow and I was able to practice a lot hitting balls off backboards when I had no one with whom to play. There were many free tennis courts and blackboards in the City of Decatur so finding an open court or backboard was not a problem. My senior year I was captain of the Decatur High School tennis team and anchored it as the sixth seated player. I was able to win a number of matches and found the game challenging and rewarding. It was like baseball in a way, played under the hot summer sun, demanding strategy, and not ruled by a clock. The big difference from baseball for me was that I was a decent player. In addition, I did not have sprained fingers at the end of a match.

There were a number of good players on the Decatur High tennis team my senior year. We went undefeated during the regular season. For regional play, the coach set up a round robin to see who was best going into the tournament. I played one of the up-and-coming sophomores. Though I gave it my best, I lost. I was upset with myself and started walking home. I took the long way back to 957 Church Street because I wanted to "cool down" mentally and physically. Unfortunately, Mrs. Renfroe, the wife of the Decatur City Schools superintendent, saw me and offered me a ride. I tried to politely decline but she insisted so I got into her car. I made polite conversation and small talk with her for almost 10 minutes, which seemed like 10 hours, with my mind somewhere else.

When we reached my house and Mrs. Renfroe let me out, I had no choice but go inside and tell my parents what had happened. I then retreated into my room and finally went out for a long walk in the cemetery. I was not going to be seen in public and the ghosts in the cemetery were quiet. My folks understood and left me alone but I stayed mad and disappointed with myself for a long time. The defeat continued to sting for the next week because I really wanted to play in the regionals. Finally, I put the loss to rest realizing there was nothing else I could do. In the end, despite the setback, I recognized I had garnered the respect of my peers over the years, earned three letters, and found a game I really loved.

CHAPTER 65

"Crunch" Beyond a Cereal and Some Rodents Other Than Mickey Mouse

Captain Crunch was a popular sugary cereal when I was growing up. We did not have it often but it affected my speech in a positive way—at least the word "crunch" did. The reason is I was looking for words other than profane ones I could say when I got angry, frustrated, flustered, disgusted, or injured. My parents seldom cussed. They got appropriately angry but never got out of control and let loose with a string of profanity. I followed their example and started using substitute words for swear words.

My first frustration word was "crunch" which was followed later by my second word "rats!" when I was really upset. The habit of saying these words stuck. I still use them and seldom say what beavers build or the informal name of solid digested food that is eliminated from the body. The Captain and some rodents changed my life or at least my speech.

CHAPTER 66

The Board of Education
or Paddling from Behind

wo Boards of Education ran Decatur High School during my time there. One was composed of civic-minded individuals who decided the physical and social policies for the school. The other belonged to Coach Thurmond. It was a paddling board—thick at the top with a good handle, the kind used in fraternity initiations. Coach Thurmond used the board to keep the boys who had physical education with him in line. It was well known that if you acted up, your bottom was going to be smacked. Some kids never learned. Most of us did. I remember one paddling and I never talked out of turn again.

Coach Thurmond acted as if he was tough but he really was a nice person. I had him for civics right after PE. One day he told me if I put a little more effort into his class, I could make an A instead of a B. That made sense to me and I gave his course an extra 10 minutes a day. It paid off. My educational experience was enriched because of his words, not the board.

CHAPTER 67

Riding Jackie Dooley
Down to the Ground

I met Jackie Dooley at the beginning of his sophomore year in high school. He was very gregarious. He lived with his mother and had a neat arrangement of having the upstairs of his house entirely to himself. It was a living situation any 15 year old boy would love.

I occasionally went to Jackie's house and hung out with him in his upstairs pad. One day several of us were at Jackie's and like typical adolescent boys, we were trading jokes and goofing off. Jackie was sitting in front of me with the 20 or so steps to the downstairs behind him. In our play, I suddenly made a lunge for him, which was meant to scare him. Instead, I hit "pay dirt." Put another way, I actually made contact with Jackie. He fell over backwards and his momentum propelled me forward. The next thing I knew I was riding Jackie like a bobsled in the Olympics and there was no stopping us. Bump, Bump, Bump—we gained speed!

In the midst of it all, I looked up. Ahead was the door to the upstairs and it was closed! I tried to say something but I was frozen in fright and could not get the words out. I knew that just as when a sleigh hits a tree, we were in for a disaster. Bam! Jackie's head hit the door and to my surprise, and relief, it flung open. However, to my dismay I went flying off Jackie and onto the floor parallel to the door for a few feet more. Neither of us was hurt but like a good Martini, we were shaken.

CHAPTER 68

Junior ROTC and Me

THE M1 THUMB AND CHEMISTRY

D ecatur High School was among a handful of high schools in the Atlanta area that had an Army Junior ROTC program. Military Science was not a required subject but most of my friends took it and my parents encouraged my brother and I to do it, too.

I got off to a rocky start in the program. The uniforms fit fine. I especially liked the "Ike" jackets from World War II but the khakis not so much. The latter were stiff and my mother had the hard job of starching and ironing them. On drill days we had rifles—M1s left over from World War II—that were much more impressive than my .22 rifle at home. We marched with the M1s and had to master the nomenclature of them, such as being "a semi-automatic, gas operated, air-cooled weapon, which holds a clip of eight rounds." Although we never fired the rifles, we were required to know how to insert the clip into the chamber and close it. Closing was tough. If you did not remove your thumb from the chamber quickly enough, the bolt would spring forward rapidly with something like forty-thousand pounds of pressure per square inch and you would get an "M1 thumb."

I am writing these words to reveal that I know what an M1 thumb feels like. My first attempt at removing my thumb from what I now call "the chamber jaws" of the rifle was unsuccessful. The result was my thumb quickly filled up with blood and throbbed like the beat of a rogue rock band. It hurt badly. Today, this type of accident would send someone to the emergency room but not then. My medical attention came from Sergeant Hacker who was always smiling, had a beard like

Richard Nixon, and had seen many M1 thumbs. After my company commander brought me into the ROTC office from the field behind the football stadium where we had drill, Sergeant Hacker immediately took over.

The remedy was to open up the thumb and get the blood out. To do so, the proper equipment was required so the good sergeant took me to the Chemistry Lab, which was not in use that period. Next, he lit a Bunsen burner and found a thin piece of copper wire. He heated the wire and instructed me to give him my thumb. I did and as I looked on, he pushed the tip of the hot wire through my thumbnail. Blood came spurting out as if he had struck the Mother Lode of a newly drilled water well. Somehow, the blood did not get on the sergeant or me but it rained down on several glass beakers. Relief came as the blood flowed forth. After the rush of the gush, it was simply a matter of covering the hole in my thumbnail by wrapping the thumb with adhesive tape. Next, the surgical sergeant and I cleaned up the mess we had made, waited for the bell to ring, and I went to my next period class.

It took a few weeks for the hole in my thumbnail to heal. Looking back, I am amazed at what Sergeant Hacker did, that my parents never questioned what went on, that school personnel never got involved, and that I never missed my next class. After the "operation," I learned to quickly remove my thumb in closing the chamber of my rifle. Fortunately, I never developed a fear of Bunsen burners or copper wire!

CHAPTER 69

An Unexpected Decoration

I have not been genuinely surprised on many occasions. The first and one of the most memorable came in the form of receiving a medal my junior year in high school. I never saw it coming.

It was honors day when the Junior ROTC distributed a number of group and individual awards and put on a competition between companies, especially in marching. I was still partially recovering from two simultaneously sprained ankles after having fallen on a slippery surface during a tennis match. The result was that while on the field with the corps, I was not nimble and definitely not swift. Nevertheless I listened, as our platoon was instructed that if our name was called during the awards ceremony we were to hand our rifle to the person next to us and quickly make our way across the football field to the bleachers where awards were being given. I did not think anything more about the instructions until I heard my name called. I was not even sure it was my name but the friends in my squad assured me it was. With that verification, I handed my rifle off and proceeded to run as fast as my sore ankles would let me across the football field.

Up ahead was a woman standing with Captain Carr, the ROTC professor of military science for the program. I stopped in front of her and parallel to him near a football goalpost and came to attention. She took two steps forward and pinned the DAR Citizenship Medal on the left pocket of my uniform as Captain Carr looked on. I did not know what to say and I simply whispered "Thank You."

That May afternoon as I walked home, my mother and Pal rode by. My mother stopped the car when she saw me and I explained what had happened as best I could. The medal came with a certificate and a voucher for having it inscribed. My mother had the engraving done at a local jewelry store the next week. I did not tell my father about the award because my mother did. Nothing more was ever said about the day or the event. Modesty was a virtue in our family. However, the weekly *Decatur-DeKalb New Era*, our county newspaper, came out with a photo of me receiving the award and a brief description below the picture stating the medal was the highest award given by the ROTC program. I am not sure they got all the facts right but the honor felt good.

CHAPTER 70

The Key to My Junior Civitan Experience

The key to my being named the outstanding member of the Junior Civitan club at Decatur High School my senior year was the Key Club. Unlike Junior Civitan which you signed up to be in and were then accepted, the Key Club was by invitation only. Boys, as it was an all-male group, received a phone call to invite them to join toward the end of their 9th grade year. The night after the calls had been made, my friend Alan Kenton asked me half in jest if I had received "a call" last night. He even winked when he said it as if he was sure I had. I replied "no." Taken aback, he realized his expectation I had been invited was incorrect. We were both embarrassed but he told me about his call and I went on to the next class feeling somewhat upset I had not made "the cut" to receive the call. As part of the Gladding tradition, I kept a stiff upper lip and did not tell anyone about my feelings.

My sophomore year I just ignored Key Club activities and went on with my life. However, my junior year, I signed up for Junior Civitan and quickly became an active member. By my senior year, I was responsible for picking up and distributing the Claxton Fruit Cakes the club sold for a fundraiser. I also encouraged club members to paint the football bleacher and do other service projects around the school and community. I think part of my energy came from having been "snubbed" my 9th grade year by the Key Club. I wanted to prove the Junior Civitan club was equal if not better, and more democratic. An expected result of my drive was that the Junior Civitian club did very well my senior year. An unexpected outcome was the recognition I received for my work. Hurt was transformed into positive actions.

CHAPTER 71

Learning to Drive and Staying Alive Through Parallel Parking

D river's Education was not a concept, let alone a class, at Decatur High School when I turned 16. Parents, guardians, friends, or paid instructors were the people who taught you to drive. I initially practiced driving with my mother but she decided the job should go to my father. I think my driving scared her and probably should have. When he had time on Sunday afternoons, after I became 15 and had a learner's permit, my dad took me to practice my driving. He went to the most remote places he could find. Putting the car in drive or reverse was easy. Parallel parking, a requirement to get a license, was much more difficult.

The first time I went to pass the driving test in our 1957 Ford Fairlane 500, I failed. The reason—I could not parallel park. "Rats!" was about all I could say. However, my father said more. Before he would take me back for a second try, I had to parallel park successfully a hundred times. I did and the good news is the next time we went to the Department of Motor Vehicles (DMV) for the test, I passed! With practice, parallel parking had become a breeze. I had mastered a skill! Even today with cars that will parallel park for you, which mine does not, I look for opportunities to back into a parking space.

CHAPTER 72

The Fuzzy Bees
and the Varsity

WHAT THE HECK, GEORGIA TECH!

S aturday night was a popular time to date in Decatur. Sometimes Decatur High had dances that anyone could attend "stag"—by yourself—or "drag"—with a date. These events were always well chaperoned. When a dance like a "sock hop"—so called because you took your shoes off and danced in your socks so you would not damage the basketball court floor—was not being held, most dating students headed down Ponce de Leon Avenue and to Atlanta. One of the favorite places to go was to see a movie at the "Fabulous" Fox Theater. The Fox was plush with large, comfortable seats, and stars on the ceiling. Before a major motion picture, Bob Van Camp would come out and play the organ. After his performance, the curtain would rise and the "News of the Day" would be shown followed by a cartoon, and finally the movie. There was a lot of entertainment for a small price. Dating couples would often see each other in the balcony. Such noting led to talk at church on Sunday or to gossip at school on Monday.

After a movie, the coolest thing to do was to go to "the Varsity," a drive-in restaurant, near Georgia Tech. The best items on the menu were the chilliDogs, Big Oranges, and fries. There was a speaker box that attached to your car window where you placed your order after which a carhop brought it out. Georgia Tech—the Yellow Jackets, or "the fuzzy bees" as I learned to call them later—was a popular school for graduates of Decatur High to attend. The Tech students frequently came to the Varsity so those of us still in high school felt mature eating at a college watering hole. The Varsity had personality. Those who took our orders or served us were sometimes quirky and surprised us with their words or behaviors.

If you had a date, Saturday was great!

CHAPTER 73

Playing the Field or
Dates by the Dozens

I f they gave out trophies for dating around, I would have had a room full by the time I finished high school. I kept hearing the message repeatedly: "Date around. Play the field." I took the message literally. In high school, I dated a girl for a while, saw what features I liked, and then moved on. Later, I conceptualized the experience somewhat akin to buying a car. I took a lot of test drives! I thought I needed to see all the models on the lot. To use another metaphor, I believed that if dating were like going to the zoo, I should see all the animals. Regardless, I actually enjoyed going out with a number of girls. Every weekend was a new adventure. Once I actually thought of going steady but the girl I liked was about as interested in me as babies are in different blends of strained spinach.

My brother did not get the date different girls memo. He dated Jean starting his junior year. He was her "Steady Ed," because nothing romantic rhymes with "Russell." They ended up going to Georgia State together and my senior year in college they married. I was his best man. After the ceremony and reception, I witnessed a bizarre and wild getaway of the newly hitched couple. Cars were chasing after each other around a rather confined parking lot with loud honking, a bit of yelling, and even one groomsman on the hood of a Buick making sounds as if he was buffalo in heat trying to mate. I had never seen such a ruckus.

A little dazed, I went to Burger King and ordered a chocolate milkshake. Since I was still in my tuxedo the casual crowd hanging out at the place that night, looked at me a bit funny. I stared back as if to say "Hey, if you guys had just witnessed what I saw—a wild and crazy car chase after a wedding—you would get more than a shake and you would not care how you looked." Of course, my stare was not translatable but I wish it had been.

If I could have a redo, I would have gone to a place that served something stronger than milkshakes, sat down at the bar, and told my story to an older and more appreciating crowd. They would have understood my frame of mind better and in mingling with them, chances are I might have run into some women who were dating around and playing the field. Then I could have relaxed!

CHAPTER 74

Double Dating

RICK ELDER AND THE HUSBAND TWINS

While some high school couples always kept to themselves, a great many of us double dated. It was less expensive and a lot of fun. For the Prom my Junior year, Rick Elder, a fellow classmate, and I decided to double. Rick played football, had been president of our class, and was in Junior Civitan. He had a white Chevy convertible with red interior. There was no question of whose car we would be taking. My parents 1957 Ford Fairlane 500 was not exactly a "chick magnet." The only unanswerable was whom we would be dating which we quickly answered: The Husband Twins! They were in the class below us and were very pretty girls. We asked them separately and both said yes. The only thing left was to pick them up on the night of the dance, which was a bit of a challenge because the driveway to their house was extremely steep—about a 110-degree angle. I do not know how their parents got a car up or down it. When we all got in the car, we were leaning forward and praying the brake was on.

The dance was a blast. I have a picture to prove it. In the picture, I am partially blond, which explains why I had so much fun that night. The reason for my blondness is that a couple of weeks before, at the state Junior Civitan conference at Jekyll Island, all the boys used peroxide to bleach their hair. The conference was also where I stuffed most of the silverware from our banquet table into Rick's sport jacket pocket. When he got up to leave, the tableware came crashing down. I am surprised he was still speaking to me on prom night.

I am sure the Husband twins easily found husbands later in life. However, on a May night in 1962 they had to settle for Rick and me.

CHAPTER 75

Carrot Walks and Talks
with Chris Hunter

My junior and senior years at Decatur High School were filled with extracurricular activities. I was a section editor of the yearbook, a class officer, on student council, a football manager, and much more. Likewise, church activities were numerous. However, one of my favorite activities had nothing to do with high school or church. It was a walk with my good friend, Chris Hunter. Chris had a vocabulary that would put a dictionary to shame. He was editor of the school newspaper, a member of the National Honor Society, and smarter than a tree full of owls. As we walked, we ate carrots. The reason we chomped on carrots instead of apples is that when Chris raided his refrigerator for our first walk, the only organic edible he found was carrots. At the end of our walks, we would bury the tops of our orange root vegetable in the front yard of Christina Westfield, a spunky girl who was cute and personable.

The walks were relaxing. Chris and I would talk about schoolwork, girls, and most importantly our impressions and reflections on what was happening in our worlds and the world at large. Occasionally, we would speculate about what we wanted to be in life. He was going to be a dentist like his father. I was going to be a minister like my grandfather. It was an exciting and anticipatory time. The memories are still good although the carrots are forever gone.

CHAPTER 76

The Studebaker and the Hairspray

My brother, Russell, was able to buy his first car in 1961 when he was a high school junior. It was a turquoise, two door, 1952 Studebaker with a choke and a stick shift. While the car was not beautiful, it was functional. It gave my brother freedom and status. It also provided a way to get to Decatur High School on time. He gave me a ride every day.

What I did not initially realize when my brother got the car is that we would not go from our house to the high school directly. Instead, we would first drive about three blocks down Church Street and pick up Diane Jacobs, who was in the class behind me. Diane was outgoing, had a pocked face, and was a member of the drill team, as was Russell's girlfriend, Jean. I would always move from the front to the back seat when we arrived at Diane's house.

The major thing I remember about our journeys was the strong smell of Diane's hair spray. The smell was not atypical of the times. Almost all high school girls had hairdos that required a lot of spray to hold them in place. In a closed space, the smell could almost be overwhelming. I remember especially in the winter months when the windows of the car were rolled up, I was very glad when my brother parked the car. It allowed me to breathe fresh air again once I got out. For the ride and for the relief in deep breathing after the journey, I will always be thankful. The Studebaker was an archetypical car for the times. I know it brought my brother much joy and multiple adventures but the rides to high school during the cold months almost asphyxiated me!

CHAPTER 77

Skiing Blindly and with Bliss

A s a teenager, I loved to water ski. Chris Hunter's parents had a cabin on Jackson Lake as well as a boat, and skis. Sometimes Chris invited me to the lake and we would spend the day on the water. My only problem on these occasions was I had a hard time getting up on the skis when the boat took off. In the midst of my struggles, a friend suggested a remedy. He said if I closed my eyes, I would concentrate better and be up on my skis quickly. Sure enough, he was right.

The first time I tried getting up with my eyes closed, I kept them closed until the boat engine stopped and those in the boat asked what I was doing, as if they questioned my sanity. I explained but they were forthright in telling me to keep my eyes open. There was scattered debris in the water and if I closed my eyes, I was likely to hit it and be hurt.

From then on, I kept my eyes closed when getting up on the skis but opened them after I had my balance. The result was I saw many "rooster tails"—an interesting name for rippled water behind a boat. I managed to jump over most of them as I followed the boat and kept a look out for the sticks, logs, frogs, and catfish as well as other skiers. Later, when sleeping I could close my eyes and picture the day. In the end, I had the best of all worlds: eyes closed, opened, and closed again.

CHAPTER 78

Mount Up-Some-More and Beyond

THE APPALACHIAN TRAIL

A t the end of two summers in my late teens, I hiked the Appalachian Trail with three of my good friends—Chris Hunter and Bob Coleman twice, and Sam Davis once. Our hikes were in Georgia and North Carolina. We took enough food for a week and enjoyed the trail and each other's company. The type of backpacks available now, were not sold then. We had to jerry-rig knapsacks to meet our needs. I remember my mother giving me sponges to put underneath the straps of my knapsack I took so they would not dig into my shoulders.

Our group, both times, was harmonious. We each took a turn leading. The rotation was smooth. We spent the nights in lean-to sheds built by the Civilian Conservation Corps back in the 1930s. Hiking the trail was not nearly as popular in the 1960s as it is today. Every night we built a fire and cooked over it. The meals were edible but forgettable. We brought a variety of foods including dried fruit and Gouda cheese for snacks. Nothing we brought needed refrigeration.

Bob, Chris, and I did the first hike—a short loop from White Oak Bottoms campground around to the top of Standing Indian and then cross-country following the Nantahala River back to the beginning. At White Oak Bottoms I was caught singing the "brusha, brusha Ipana" toothpaste song by strangers. I was a little embarrassed especially considering I did not have good teeth or a melodious singing voice. The last night we all slept in the car because there were not any cabins available. It is not anything I would recommend—that is sleeping in the car.

The second trip was with Chris, Bob, Sam Davis, a football player who would later star at Vanderbilt and die young from cancer at age 33, and me. It was a longer hike that ended at Stecoah Gap. I kept a diary on this trip and invented "Mount Up-Some-More" for a mountain that had another name but seemed to go up forever. Highlights of the trip included field mice making a nest of toilet paper in Sam Davis's pants, playing football using sand in a baggie for a ball, and Sam Davis's father picking us up at the end of our journey and bringing us back home. We all slept.

When we finished both hikes, we had only a week or two before college. My peers on the trail taught me a lot about nature, groups, traveling on foot, and life. From the wild I became more civilized.

CHAPTER 79

Doing 90 Miles an Hour
down a Dead End Street

E very year at Decatur First Baptist, the congregation observed
Youth Week. It was when senior high youth "took over," in name
only, the positions of the church staff. The one exception was the
youth named as minister. He, and it was always a he in the 1960s, had
to preach sermons on Sunday evening one week and Sunday morning
the next. As expected, I was named youth pastor my senior year. Actually, it was in my senior year that the two-sermon requirement came
into effect.

I did unexpectedly well on the Sunday night event. My sermon
topic was "Doing 90 miles an hour down a dead end street." I lifted
the title from a song I heard only once on the radio—WAKE, 1340 AM.
Since I did not know all the words, I made a few up. The first verse went:

I took you home from a date last night
And all the stars were shinning bright
But instead of stopping where we should have
We went right on
Until suddenly we found the brakes were gone.
Now warning signs keep flashing by us but we pay no heed,
Instead of slowing down the pace, we keep picking up the speed
Disaster getting closer, soon it we will meet
Doing 90 miles an hour down a dead end street.

The point of the sermon was to be aware and not race down dead
end paths. Somehow, I tied it all together even using the lyrics in the

Sound of Music song "You are sixteen going on seventeen, Baby it's time to think!"

The second sermon was on exploration and although I cannot remember the title, the homily centered on looking for faith like the Spanish explorer Coronado searched for gold in the American west.

I received numerous compliments, especially for the first sermon. Even my father conveyed to friends how surprised he was at how well I did. It was rare for him to talk about any of his children in public. Regardless, my career as a minister was off to a good start. Looking back, those sermons may have been the highlight of the religious road I was on.

CHAPTER 80

"And This Shall Be a Sign unto You"

There were a number of ways to show a girl at Decatur High that you liked her. Probably the best way was just to tell her. However, for those of us with fewer social skills, there was an alternative. It was to put a real estate sign in her front yard. If you really liked the girl, a couple of signs were better yet and the word would get around that you were "signing on" to an interest in her.

One girl I liked went beyond the two signs limit. I am not sure why I thought this young woman was so special but if I could get back into my 16-year-old brain, I am sure I could figure it out. Whatever the reason, with the help of some friends I gathered five real estate signs and around 11 p.m. put the signs on her front lawn. We had to be as quiet as mice but we managed.

Smug and satisfied, I started to drive my co-conspirators home. Just a block from the scene of our Saturday night adventure, blue lights flashed and a siren came from the car behind me. It was the City of Decatur police. I was nervous as a cat in a room full of rocking chairs but showed the officer my driver's license and car registration. He looked suspiciously at my three friends and me. He followed his look with a rather stern voice: "Better get home boys. I have been watching you drive around this neighborhood a lot tonight." What he did not say was "And I saw you put the real estate signs in a yard." Fifteen minutes later, we were all home.

My mother was in the living room reading her Sunday School lesson when I walked in. She just nodded and asked how my evening had been. I said "fine" careful not to say the word "sign." I thought to myself "Thank God" I was not caught signing or I would have been in serious trouble—not so much with the police but with my mother!

CHAPTER 81

Hauling Fruitcake and Flipping Paint

In a previous vignette, I may have highlighted my experience in Junior Civitan in colors that were too rosy. I liked the club and the people in it but I did have some near and actual mishaps with the club. For instance, I almost ruined the backend of our 1957 Ford Fairlane when I persuaded my mother to go with me to pick up the club's allotment of Claxton Fruit Cakes members sold around Christmas time. Our order was more than I imagined. When it had been loaded in our car's trunk, the rear end suspension was definitely straining. The car looked like it could have been hauling moonshine. Fortunately, after our haul was unloaded the car reverted to its regular shape. No harm was done.

However, my major mishap with Junior Civitan came toward the end of school. As implied earlier, I was heavily involved in the club's decision to paint the fading football bleachers. The color chosen was a forest green. Some members worked on Saturdays. Others painted after school. As I waited for one of the latter groups to arrive and get the supplies I had bought, I became bored. Rather than sit down and be patient, I started flipping a can of paint I had previously held upright. I was wearing my tennis togs that were all white because we had a match that day. The first few times I flipped the paint can, all went well. About the eighth time though, the can went through my hands, hit the ground with a bang as the top came off. "Splash!" I was now wearing white above my knees and green below. The asphalt in front of the school was now green and black. My slip up had changed the color of the environment and my outlook on the day as well.

Almost at the same time of the accident, the painting students arrived. I smiled, told them to be careful, and walked gingerly to a grassy area nearby where I did my best to get clean. I partially succeeded, played the tennis match later looking a bit odd, and arrived home to find my parents displeased with my appearance. Turpentine stayed on my body and mind for some time afterwards. I had to use a lot on my legs before they were restored to their natural color. I wish I had been a bit more flippant and a lot less clumsy!

CHAPTER 82

Radiating Fruit Flies

Every year students who took a science course at Decatur High School had to do a science project. Those of us not gifted with scientific minds always scrambled to come up with a project that would not hurt our already fragile grades. I took chemistry my junior year and was determined to get ahead on my project before the science fair came around in February. I knew nothing about how to experiment with chemicals so I dropped back to biology. Charles Darwin and his theories fascinated me and I decided to do something on mutations. I needed an organism that reproduced quickly and that I could easily handle. The answer: fruit flies.

I sent off to a lab in North Carolina for several jars of fruit flies. When they arrived, I bought bananas and set up new colonies from the pupa that came in the original jars. The life cycle of the flies was a few weeks and they were active breeders. I wondered what radiation would do if the flies were exposed to it while still in a cocoon state. My hypothesis was they might come out with more than two eyes or the color of their eyes might change. Fortunately, my friend Chris Hunter's dad was a dentist and he offered to expose my flies to the x-ray machine in his office. I made three trips to see him.

I did not win a prize for my work but my grade did not suffer either. Happily, the fruit flies were no worse for wear either—none of their eyes or wings changed. The only negative in the experiment was that some of the "subjects" escaped and made themselves at home. Our house had fruit flies around for several weeks longer than my project. My parents thought we could outlast the inconvenience and did not call an exterminator. My mother simply did not buy bananas for a few weeks.

CHAPTER 83

The Gun and the Legacy

In a locked drawer beneath the secretary desk in Pal and Peggy's room, where I studied most nights in high school, was a handgun. It had belonged to my maternal grandfather Samuel Huntington Templeman. The sheriff in Laurens, South Carolina, gave it to him after he helped stop a lynching. The sheriff thought some of the men in the group might try to take revenge on my grandfather, who was the minister of the First Baptist Church in Laurens, and who had a young family.

As far as I know, my grandfather came home from the incident that night and locked the gun in the drawer. It was never fired. Whether he meant for it to become a symbol of his bravery or not, it did.

CHAPTER 84

Mafia in Piedmont Park

My friends and I, when dateless one Saturday night, played Mafia or as we called it "dead body." We only played it once and that was enough! The game consisted of having one of us, not me because I was the driver, get into the trunk of our 1957 Ford Fairlane 500. We then drove to Piedmont Park in Atlanta, which was the official lover's lane of the city, i.e., you could park and make out. No one was supposed to disturb you.

On the occasion, which was my junior year in high school, we drove up in front of a heavily fogged windowed car. As we stopped, the three guys who were with me in the passenger seats quickly got out, opened the trunk, and took the limp body of our other co-conspirator out and dumped it on the grass. Afterwards, they quickly got back in the car and we sped away. Our friend on the grass rolled down the hill from the side of the road and in the darkness sprang to his feet, ran, and met us a few hundred yards away at a bend in the road. The first time we played the Mafia game, we did not get any reaction. The second time we played, a girl in the car behind us screamed. After the scream, we never played the game again. We were too scared and more importantly even at 16 we realized how socially stupid we had been!

CHAPTER 85

"I'm a Worm"

A SONG WITH JERRY EICKHOFF ON A RAINY DAY

A fter a long stretch of rain, my friend, Jerry Eickhoff, whose family lived on my paper route, suggested we do something fun that did not involve a lot of physical activity since the ground was saturated. He played guitar and so we joined together to make up a song. It was called "I'm a Worm" and had a slow tempo, something like a 2/4 beat. It was sung to the sound of snapping fingers.

I was born in the ground, didn't have no light
With a bunch of wiggles and squirms
I saw my brother who gave me a fright
I lived in a family of worms!

Chorus

I'm a worm, I'm a worm,
And I'll never be no taller,
I come from a noble family of worms
I'm a right nice size, night crawler.
My mother died when I was three
A fact that makes me sick,
Some smart alec kid didn't see her head
Sticking out of the apple he picked!

Chorus

My old man was a real hip cat
He could dance and boogaloo all day

But all I know of him is rumors
'Cause he's in the belly of a Bluejay

Chorus

I was layin' around on top of the ground
Trying to get me a tan
When I felt two fingers around my side
I ended up in an old coffee can
Then I felt a terrible pain in my side
And I was down in water dark as night
When I saw two eyes looking up at me
And heard the man say: "I got a bite."

New Chorus

I was a worm! I was a worm!
And if I had one last wish,
If there's such a thing as reincarnation
I want to come back as a big fish!

CHAPTER 86

Senior Year Officer

A t Decatur High School in the 1960s, you could volunteer for service projects but you could not nominate yourself for an office of any organization. The process was one where fellow students would write your name down if they thought you should be in a leadership position. I had been a student council representative in the 8th grade but had not been nominated for anything since. Therefore it surprised and pleased me when I was nominated and elected to be a representative to student council from my homeroom my senior year. I was even more astonished a few days later when I was one of eight boys nominated to be class treasurer. My peers had never nominated me for a class office before. The list of eight was reduced to three in a second round of voting and again to my amazement, I was in the top three. A few days later on a Friday afternoon, it was announced I had been elected.

While being a class officer is not the highest honor in the world, especially being class treasurer, I was thrilled and walked a little lighter for a few days. It was an affirmation. I strove hard that year to live up to the responsibility. Interestingly, my peers also elected me treasurer of the Junior Civitan Club and the Junior ROTC Officers Club. I was awash in cash!

CHAPTER 87

Mr. McCurdy and the "Ole Baldy" Sunday School Lessons

M r. McCurdy was one of the most prominent attorneys in town. His office was right off the courthouse square in Decatur. He helped me pass my Boy Scout Citizenship merit badges. My senior year in high school, he was my Sunday School teacher at the First Baptist Church. I do not remember any of his specific lessons except almost all of them had to do with people he had worked with in the judicial system, mostly criminals. One character who seemed to consistently reappear in the lessons was "Ole Baldy." I guess he got in trouble a lot.

Mr. McCurdy combined his stories of men in trouble with the importance of values and lessons from the Bible. I have never met a finer man or heard religious lessons that were more unusual and inspiring. I doubt I ever will.

CHAPTER 88

The Legacy of Miss Lewis

Miss Lewis must have been somewhere in her 30s when I met her. She was both my homeroom teacher and my Senior English teacher at Decatur High School. She was not a beauty queen but she was attractive and had an award-winning personality. She was naturally pleasant, naturally shy, and her standards were as high as Atlanta's skyscrapers. I worked hard in her class and made mostly B's with an occasional sprinkling of A's. She encouraged me as a writer and was particularly supportive of my poetry.

One day she came in with a trophy and announced it would be given to the district winner of the Voice of Democracy essay contest. For some reason I associated the trophy with Miss Lewis and a couple of days before the deadline, I wrote my essay on what democracy meant to me and handed it in. The next week it was announced I had won. The contest was a bigger event than I thought. A Veteran of Foreign Wars leader presented me with the trophy as Miss Lewis and Mr. Purcell, the school principal, looked on. A picture of the presentation appeared in the local paper and I recorded my essay for a local radio station.

While I received this award and some recognition thanks to Miss Lewis that is not what I took away from my senior year in her class. Rather, I realized through Miss Lewis that a teacher could have high standards and yet be enjoyable and encouraging. I have been grateful for what she taught me ever since and have tried to emulate her in my teaching.

CHAPTER 89

Introducing the Football Managers

I became a football manager during my sophomore year in high school. I did not like sitting in the bleachers at football games. I could not see the field that well. Being a football manager put me where the action was. I enjoyed carrying the equipment and taking water to the boys on the field during time outs. Handing out vitamin C and salt tablets after practice was an exercise in encouragement and health. I made some good friends during all of these activities. My parents were always in the stands on Friday nights when we had a home game. I think they took pride in what their youngest son was doing.

My most notable time as a football manager came my senior year. We had a new coach, Franklin Brooks, who had been an All American at Georgia Tech. He was not as personable or as skilled at paying attention to details off the field as the old coach, Charlie Hall, who after leaving Decatur High became a respected history teacher at DeKalb Community College. When the high school had an assembly to recognize the football team, Coach Brooks did not know the names of the managers except for me. Therefore, he asked me to introduce them.

I had listened to the way the football player were introduced, such as "Paul Jones, a junior linebacker, 6 foot 2 inches, 170 pounds, fast as greased lightning—a favorite phrase of the time—and a potential All State candidate." Following that formula, I began my introduction of the managers in a similar way. "I'd like to introduce you to Dan McKinney. Dan is 5 foot 7 inches and probably weighs 130 pounds after a good rain. Dan's specialty is taping ankles and handing out socks. He is not fast at doing either but we think Dan has potential in both areas and we are counting on him to pick up speed as the year goes on."

We had four managers and by the end of the introductions, the serious nature of the event had been transformed into a comedy. My classmates enjoyed it and even the cheerleaders gave me compliments. However, Coach Brooks never said a word. He was as chatty as a stone in Antarctica. Rather quickly, he learned the names of the managers and never had me introduce them again.

CHAPTER 90

Cool Breeze

A LESSON IN THE TRAGEDY OF RACISM

As a high school football manager, I worked with the other managers to take care of the team's equipment and clean up after the players went home. On Saturday mornings during the season, we straightened up the locker room as well as did some of the team's laundry. While we waited for the dryers to finish, my fellow managers and I would play games of touch football out on the field that had been the center of attention the night before. Sometimes we played among ourselves, all white Decatur High boys. At other times, African American kids from the Black high school—Trinity—would join us. We always had a spirited interracial game.

My favorite player on either side of the ball was a 15-year-old Black boy about my age known as "Cool Breeze." He earned the name because of his speed. He was faster than a gazelle being chased by a lion. Whether going up the middle or around the end, we seldom could catch him. He would dart past and afterwards we would feel the "cool breeze" of the air which was left in his wake. He was "awesome"—a natural athlete!

As great as "Cool Breeze" was on the field, his life and success were later not as good. He did not have many choices educationally, socially, and vocationally. He was caged in, relegated to a life style that restricted his movement and ambition because of segregation. What could have been never was. The mindset of the day kept people "down" and prevented possibilities.

Whenever I think of the time and the life of "Cool Breeze," it makes me sad and mad. Life is too valuable to waste and individuals are too important to treat like chattel. If there is one action privileged people can do, it is to open up possibilities and opportunities. While openings do not guarantee success, without options individuals usually get caught in failure.

CHAPTER 91

Marrying Mickey Johnson

The 1960s was a decade of traditions and stereotypes. As Archie Bunker would say in the 1970s television series *All in the Family*, "girls were girls and men were men." Therefore, having a skit about a womanless wedding was considered funny. The same would not be seen in the same way today.

A number of the boys in our senior class staged the skit with each dressing his appropriate part as a man or woman in a wedding party. I was the groom at 115 pounds. Mickey Johnson, who must have weighed close to 200 pounds, was the bride. I am not sure where Mickey found a dress that would fit him. I can assure you, he did not look radiant coming down the aisle in the gym. He just looked large! I was glad our pretend vows were exactly that! To have spent a honeymoon with Mickey would have crushed me!

CHAPTER 92

Typing

A MORNING EXERCISE

I was not able to get a job between graduating from high school and going to college. While I would usually play tennis in the afternoon and go out with friends at night, my mornings were free and after a few days, they were boring. My parents had bought me a typewriter. The only trouble was, I could not type. In the early 1960s, keyboarding was for girls so they could get a job as a secretary, if needed.

I found a book on typing around our house that had belonged to my mother when she was an adolescent. One morning I put my index fingers on the "G" and the "H" in the second row of letters and expanded from there as I followed the instructions on how to type. It became a post-breakfast ritual. By the end of the summer, I could type three pages an hour as long as I kept my eyes on the keys. It was not much but it was further than I had been. Months later, it saved me the expense of having someone type my college papers. Unemployment and discipline paid rich dividends.

CHAPTER 93

Goodbye Church Street; Hello Lamont Drive

The summer of 1963 was an extremely busy one for my family. It involved moving, as my father purchased a new house on Lamont Drive for my mother. Moving meant leaving the house on Church Street our family had lived in for over 20 years. In the midst of the intracity move was my interstate transport to college.

What sparked our family's move that summer was my father's income and desire. He was actually making a good income after years of just getting by. He was determined to make everything up to my mother for the lean times they had shared together. His first order of business was buying a better house. Our abode on Church Street had been fine in many respects for although cramped; it had fostered cooperation and understanding. For instance, my brother and I had to realize that neither of us could "hog the covers" on the bed we shared. Three bedrooms and one bath meant teamwork and coordination were essential. However, saying goodbye to Church Street was difficult for me. I had grown up in the house and even realizing we were not affluent, I took some pride in having made the best of our situation and having overcome some difficulties. When the moving truck came, I was ambivalent. My feelings ranged from nostalgia for the past to hopefulness for the future. I was also realistic in knowing I would only spend summer vacations and academic breaks on Lamont Drive. I was pleased my parents, siblings, and Pal would live a better life though.

On moving day a young woman, who went by the nickname "Sister," whom I had had had a frustrating dating relationship with, came to our house on Church Street and brought me a belated graduation present. It was a small, all-purpose jewelry box, in which I could keep tie tacks, rings, pins, and other small objects. I was grateful. It was a nice way to end a relationship. We were both moving on.

After the moving truck left with our furniture, we made at least a dozen trips back to Church Street to pick up plants, pots, and other miscellaneous items that had not been loaded on the van. Finally settled in, I enjoyed our new place for about six weeks before it was time to go to college. I had my own bed on Lamont Drive and the house had central air conditioning. It was much roomier and had a lightness about it that was unexplainable and positively different. I was glad for my family but I stayed a perpetual visitor and forever a product of Church Street.

PART IV

College (18–21 Years Old)

Young adulthood usually is considered to be between 18 and 34, but this last section will only cover the four-year period of traditional college life for those who enter college at 18. Technically, I began my journey into this domain a few months early. I was about a month shy of being 18 when I went off to college. I vividly remember registering to vote and applying for an absentee ballot during my first semester away from home. As I look back, I had more fervor than insight at the time. I had loved John F. Kennedy but I was not enthralled with Lyndon Johnson. Therefore, I registered as a Republican and voted for Barry Goldwater, even though Johnson supported everything I believed in, e.g., voting rights and social programs. I am still embarrassed about who I voted for although I am proud I took the time and made the effort to vote as soon as I was eligible.

My father stressed early that it was important to get a college education, something he did not have because of the Great Depression. He also emphasized I needed to take advantage of opportunities with his famous one line that "you can't be a promising young man forever." I took him at his word. Unfortunately, I did not receive any guidance, other than college fairs, about college. Uninformed, I went forward.

CHAPTER 94

Off to College and Being "off" in My Choice

STETSON

I began my college career at Stetson University in DeLand, Florida. I had only been to Florida—Daytona Beach—once, a few months before I matriculated at Stetson. I remember thinking it was hotter than what I was accustomed to, flat, sandy, and the main environmental features were Palm Trees and Spanish moss that hung from the oak trees. In other words, I had no idea that central Florida was going to be so different from northern Georgia.

I chose Stetson because it was a Baptist school and I had been told countless times I should attend a Baptist college since I was planning to be a minister. My high school counselors saw me as mature and thought I knew what I was doing. They did not call me in to talk with them about colleges. The only instructions I received about college were from well-meaning people who did not consider how I would fit within a particular institution of higher learning. My choice of Stetson could not have been more wrong.

My first impressions of the University were mixed. Stetson played soccer instead of football in the fall. Few students cared about soccer and even fewer attended games. There was practically no school spirit. My assessment of the buildings was that most were old but functional, the exceptions being the student center and some of the men's dorms which were newer. The campus was divided between Greeks and independents. There was virtually no social life outside the Greek system.

My classmates, who were predominantly Floridians, had different customs and habits than I had. For example, my first year roommate was a smart and friendly guy who later went on to graduate school. However, being a south Floridian, he had a way of dressing—or not—that freaked me out initially. He would hang around in his underwear, at least in our room. It was his way of staying cool because the dorms were not air-conditioned. We got along fine, kept regular hours, ate meals together, walked to class and talked together. We were two of the three on a hall of 30, who actually went up quality points after the first semester. Still, I was ambivalent as to how close I wanted to be with him.

The person I most identified with was another native Floridian, John Tubb, who was more similar to me than anyone I met and with whom I roomed my sophomore year. I am sure Stetson was a fine school when I matriculated. It was just a mismatch between the institution and me. It took me a while to figure out the problem but I did and transferred at the end of my sophomore year.

CHAPTER 95

The Daily Bailey

I hated pop tests when I was in college and I still dislike them intensely. However, for some sadistic reason they were popular with professors in the 1960s. My most hated—do you get the impression I did not like pop quizzes?—was what my friends and I infamously called "The Daily Bailey." It was administered my first year of college at 8 a.m. in the morning by my history professor, Dr. Bailey. I will not use his first name to protect the innocent. Once a week for the year I had him, he gave a pop quiz on the readings assigned for the day.

I had his class on Tuesday, Thursday, and Saturday. Yes, there were Saturday classes in the 1960s. While I often did well on these tests, I was sometimes stumped. Preparing for his "pops" kept me up in history, kept me up at night, and kept me from studying some of my other subjects in as much depth as I would have liked.

Going Greek

OH, IF THERE HAD ONLY BEEN ROMANS!

C ampus life at Stetson was as placid as any lake in Florida. Another word for life on campus was "dull." It depended on your perspective and your involvement in activities. Besides the campus flicks on Friday or Saturday nights, there was not a lot to do as a first year student if you were not in a fraternity or sorority. Realizing this fact, I decided I would go Greek. However, the Greeks decided otherwise. I had been popular in high school so I had some confidence when I went out for "Rush." There were eight fraternities with about 40 to 50 guys in each so I thought, "No problem." Maybe I should have thought again. The first time I rushed in the fall semester of my first year, I did not receive an invitation back to any of the houses let alone a bid to join one of the groups. I was amazed, shocked and frankly hurt. Determined, I rushed two more times in the spring semester of my first year and in the fall semester of my sophomore year. History repeated itself. Ouch! I did not understand why. To make matters worse, no one seemed to care except for me.

It did not occur to me until years later that I may have lacked "packaging," that is, height. At 5′ 2″, I was not of average height and for men in fraternities at Stetson, and probably many other places, average height was the first step in having your ticket punched to join. Thus, my stature probably ruled me out from being a part of the Greek system. The pictures of the groups in the yearbooks of the time seem to back up my hypothesis . . . although let's face it, maybe I had bad breath!

In hindsight, I must have been seen like a barbarian to the Greeks. I did not understand the system. I blamed myself but carried on in my family's tradition of keeping a stiff upper lip. I made my grades, wrote for the student newspaper and worked on a committee of the Student Union. Outside of these activities, I had a less than desirable college life. I decided to transfer because it was just too painful being a Hatter. As I got ready to leave at the end of my second year at Stetson, I was one of three non-Greeks inducted into the sophomore men's leadership honorary: The Green Circle. It was a nice recognition but . . . it did nothing for me socially. I wish there had been a Roman alternative to the Greek system.

CHAPTER 97

Jumpin' Jehoshaphat

THE PREACHERS!

The Preachers was the name of a student organization at Stetson composed of men who were headed to seminary to become Baptist pastors. There were about 30 members of the group. The members as a whole seemed a bit narrow in their outlooks on life serving the church with the exception of a few upperclassmen who were more open-minded but in the minority. Regardless, the Preachers were well-organized holding Bible studies and fielding intramural athletic teams. While the Bible studies were fine, the athletic endeavors were for the most part less than divine. God was not on their side and miraculous victories did not occur!

After a few meetings, I realized I was having trouble identifying with the group. I wanted to think what was going on was an anomaly but it was reality. I had little in common with most of the members and so I only attended meetings occasionally and finally not at all. My experience with the Preachers was the first time I thought I might not be cut out to be a minister. Jumpin' Jehoshaphat! With my social life at rock bottom and everything else less than stellar, but my grades, I could see my life at Stetson was going south . . . and not to Miami!

CHAPTER 98

Qué Pasa

SPANISH

S tetson had some good professors. One of them was Dr. Gerald Anderson who taught Spanish and did not give pop tests. In an earlier reflection, I mentioned my command of the English language was suspect. Trying to pick up Spanish was made more difficult by that fact.

Dr. Anderson mainly spoke Spanish in class and gave thorough tests. In giving back quizzes, the best grades were always on the top of his stack. My quizzes were most often on the bottom. Yet, as hard as he was, Dr. Anderson was kind. He talked to me on several occasions on how to study Spanish and how to prepare for his tests. He seemed concerned. While I was studying hard before, I doubled down and studied even harder. I had a tape recorder that played Spanish words for me before going to sleep. When I woke up, I turned the recorder back on as I got dressed. My Spanish textbook and I closed down the library on a number of occasions. As my minister would say about Baptism, I was "immersed." Everything came down to the final exam my first semester. It was somewhat like when a basketball game comes down to the last shot. My determination and hard work paid off. I passed the course by a point. Unfortunately, there was not a court to rush or a net to cut down. Still, I was elated! I wanted to cheer "Spanish!" "Spanish!" "Spanish!"

Dr. Anderson taught me that professors could be tough as nails and as helpful as hammers. It was a valuable lesson to learn . . . maybe even more important than mastering Spanish.

CHAPTER 99

A June Night in December

June Gay was a pretty, young woman who was a class behind me at Decatur High School. She lived on Vidal Boulevard, which was a much classier residential neighborhood than Church Street. Her family went to the same church as my family. However, I did not see her that much because of the large number of students in my class and in hers. We were part of the Baby Boom generation following World War II. I had a date with June during Twirp Week in high school, when girls could ask boys out, but somehow we just never connected.

Then came my first year in college and June's senior year in high school. We wrote some and I realized anew how clever she was. In November, she invited me to the "Snow Ball" which was a dance at Decatur High in December that was always devoid of snow. I accepted and looked forward to the night. I picked her up and all went well until in closing the door for her, I accidentally shut it on her hand. By the time I got around to my side of the car, the damage had been done. Instead of spending a romantic night dancing, we spent the night in the emergency room of a local hospital where June got stitched up. I felt terrible. I had hurt a nice girl and I had blown what promised to be a great evening or even a future.

I tried to make up for my actions, even writing June a poem. However, there was really no recovery. George Washington is purported to have said "Great moments in love and great moments in war should always be made the most of for they never come again." I do not know about war but I am sure the father of our country was right about love.

CHAPTER 100

The Death of Pal

Pal's death came during the last two weeks of the spring semester my sophomore year at Stetson. She was 87 and had been bedridden for several months after having suffered a number of strokes. Her passing was actually a blessing.

However, her death meant arrangements had to be made. There was a memorial service in Decatur and a service and burial in Richmond. My first task was to get to Decatur. I did not have a choice but to fly. As soon as I found out that she had died, I took a bus from DeLand to Jacksonville and flew out that night arriving after midnight in Atlanta. My father picked me up and we did not reach home and get to bed until around 2 a.m. It was another couple of days before the memorial service. In that time a number of church members and neighbors came by and the family was kept busy greeting, interacting with, and thanking them for their thoughtfulness and food.

After the service in Decatur, we hit the road for Richmond. It was a long car ride. My attention for most of the trip, still riding the hump, was how spring foliage disappeared the further north we drove. Richmond was not in bloom. Decatur was. We stayed at the house of my Aunt Mildred and Uncle Alan. At the visitation, I met members of the Templeman family I did not know existed. They were on the shorter side of tall and I felt like they were my people.

Before the memorial service, I remember my dad instructing my brother and me to be strong, which meant not to cry. I am afraid I did not pass that test. After the service, Pal was buried next to her husband, Samuel. They had been separated by death for 19 years.

I left Richmond with multiple thoughts. I was sad about Pal's death as well as anxious about having missed an entire week of classes just one week before the semester ended. Spring unfolded as we drove back to Atlanta. Amidst it all, I felt a strange sense of calm. What was to happen next was in my hands and I thought of how my grandmother in her healthier time would have handled it. I had no doubt she would face it head on, let it develop, and come out okay.

Although this chapter in the life of our family had ended, it was not the last I saw of Pal. Approximately eight year later when I was in the midst of a depression over an engagement that was my fault in ending; I had another encounter with Pal. It was in a dream. I was crawling through a desert and wondering if I was going to die. As I struggled, a group of my ancestors, led by her suddenly appeared. She was with my maternal grandfather, Samuel Templeman, and others I could not immediately recognize but who I know cared about me. Pal's words were simple. "We will carry you until you can walk by yourself." With that, the group gently lifted me up and started carrying me on their shoulders. I woke up and realized that though I was in psychological pain, I would eventually be all right. Pal's reemergence with my historical relatives reassured me of my ability to move on and gave me hope. It probably saved my life.

CHAPTER 101

Off to College and Being "on" in my Choice

WAKE FOREST

O nce I realized Stetson and I were mismatched, I began to explore where to transfer. By chance, I talked with a good high school friend, Ed Hallman who was a first year student at Wake Forest. Ed seemed very happy at "the Forest." He described the Atlantic Coast Conference college as "the next best place to heaven." My religious training made me think this college might be a good fit. It was.

Wake Forest had a lot of school spirit and excellent academics. Students were welcoming, friendly, and accepting. I realized I was in my element starting with the pre-school retreat at Camp Hanes where there were three days of dancing, swimming, co-ed softball games, hikes up Sauratown Mountain, and programs emphasizing spirituality and a reverence for life. In the lyrics from an Elvis Presley song, I was "all shook up" but in a good and positive way.

CHAPTER 102

Grandfathers and Roommates

I was assigned a roommate at Wake Forest. I did not have a choice. When the assignment came in July of 1965, my roommate turned out to be Jeff Kincheloe, a sophomore from Rocky Mount, North Carolina. My mother, upon hearing the word "Kincheloe," perked up. Her father had roomed with Jeff's grandfather at Richmond College in the early part of the 20th century. They had both become Baptist ministers.

Lean, tall, handsome, soft spoken and articulate, Jeff and I ended up being good roommates and friends. He was smarter—at least more philosophical—than I was. We were both active in College Union and ROTC. I never did the math on what the odds were that the grandsons of two roommates from another era and a different college would be assigned randomly to room together but I think the chances were, and are, slim. Our assigned pairing seemed to me to be another sign Wake Forest was meant to be in my life.

CHAPTER 103

Room 308 and the Maids

I roomed in 308 Taylor Dorm both my junior and senior years at Wake Forest. It was an interesting setup. The room had formerly been a lounge for the maids who serviced the men's residence hall. It had a narrow entrance with an elongated hall that opened up at the end with two windows. A bathroom was off to the left as you made your way down the hall. As oddly shaped as the room was, it housed a bunk bed and two desks. Most rooms in the dorms for men on the Quad had a hallway with four rooms off it and a bathroom at the end.

My dorm room was the first year a maids' lounge had been converted into student housing. Yes, oddly enough Wake Forest had room cleaning service in the men's dorms until the early 1970s. Two maids came during the day to tidy up our rooms and make our beds. It is still a mystery to me how maid service ever started. Men must have been considered unable or unwilling to keep neat rooms. Women had no such service. They were generally smarter than men at Wake Forest at the time, i.e., they had higher SAT scores, and they also had dorm mothers, i.e., older single women who lived with them in the residence halls. Overall, they must have also been considered more capable. In the early 1970s, the maids were phased out. By then, I think Wake Forest must have started admitting more domesticated males.

CHAPTER 104

The Lakes of Wake
and Other Stories

PUB ROW, HUMOR, AND SHYNESS

I was the athletic section editor of the *Howler*, the Wake Forest year-book, my junior year so I spent a lot of time on "Pub Row" an abbreviation for Publication Row where the yearbook, student newspaper, radio station, and literary magazine were all housed on the 3rd floor of Reynolda Hall. I enjoyed laying out the pages and writing the copy. Yet, I wanted to write humorous pieces too and the literary magazine, *The Student*, was a natural outlet for that.

One day, while sitting at my favorite desk on the fourth floor of the Z. Smith Reynolds Library near a window, where I could watch the sun set and get inspired to write, I decided to go for it—write a humorous essay. "The Lakes of Wake" was my first attempt. It was a rainy day and I noticed the campus had poor drainage. Inspired by what I saw, I wrote about the ponds of water that formed. After writing the essay in long hand, I spent about three hours typing it. When it was finished, I was too shy to deliver it to the editor even though I knew him. I waited until I was sure everyone had left the Row. Under cover of darkness, I slid my essay under the editor's door. To my delight, I received an acceptance letter a few days later in my campus mailbox. The editor conveyed he thought my writing was "deft." I did not know the meaning of the word but was thrilled when I looked it up.

My feet did not touch the ground for a few days because it had rained again and the lakes had reformed. Upcoming tests and essays brought me back to reality. Having my work accepted boosted my creative confidence. Still I waited past midnight when no one was around to submit the next piece of humor I wrote. It was on toilet paper, uh, the practice of throwing it in the trees after an athletic victory.

CHAPTER 105

Student Government

A MOVING EXPERIENCE

I decided to run to be a legislator in the Student Government during the spring semester of my junior year. At the time, I did not anticipate being heavily involved in other Wake Forest activities my senior year. I also thought being a part of Student Government would be a lot of fun and I might positively influence the campus. Thus, I signed up with one of the two parties that sponsored candidates: the BPOC (Better Politics on Campus).

I won and enthusiastically volunteered to be chair of the Transportation Committee. My job in this role was to line up bus transportation for football games, which were played across town at Bowman Gray Stadium, and for basketball games at Memorial Coliseum. The task was not hard. I just had to make a few phone calls to the Safe Bus Company and be in front of the south campus dorms when the buses arrived to make sure everyone got on board.

In the midst of the football season, I decided to be adventuresome and schedule a bus caravan to an away game. My caravan ended up consisting of one bus, 35 students, to Charlottesville to see the Virginia-Wake Forest football game in the fall of 1966. I had lined up box lunches for the group so no one went hungry. We lost but everyone seemed to have a good time. Food mitigated the pain of losing and it was a unique experience watching Virginia fans sing "Auld Lang Syne" after the game.

At the end of the school year, I received the award for being the best Student Government committee chair. It was a loving cup—a popular way of recognizing people at the time. I still have the cup and when looking at it, I wonder if I did a stellar job or if no one else did much. Regardless, I enjoyed being a legislator. Laminated on one of the tables at Shorty's in the Benson Center at Wake Forest is a picture of our Student Government class for 1966–1967. I always sit at that table when I can. It brings back good memories.

CHAPTER 106

The Baptists, the Banana, and the BSU

When I entered Wake Forest as a junior, I still intended to be a Baptist minister. Wake had tons of Baptists on campus. The *Winston-Salem Journal* even reported there were more Baptists than people in North Carolina. The Baptist Student Union (BSU) was quite large and active.

I joined the BSU almost immediately. My first activity with the group was visiting a retirement community once a week. Most of the visits went fine but one time I was holding an older woman's hand who was laying on her back and had a very tight grip. It was time to go and I was having a hard time getting free. For some reason, it occurred to me I could probably slip a banana, from the fruit bowl on her table, into where my hand was and all would be fine. I did. The next week when I visited her, she did not say anything about the week before. I assume she fell asleep with the banana and woke up not remembering our encounter.

However, most of my activities with the BSU were more stimulating and enlightening. They included off-campus retreats, Vespers at 6 p.m. in Davis Chapel, putting together an irregular newsletter titled "Breakthrough," and monthly BSU dinners whose menus included food for thought as well as food for substance.

In the spring of my junior year, new officers of the BSU were scheduled to be elected. I was not on the ballot but planned to attend the meeting and vote. To my surprise, about an hour before the meeting I received a call asking if I would run for president of the group. A petition had been started with my name at the top. Apparently, the two candidates on the ballot were not ringing anyone's chimes or the Chapel bells. "Okay," I said, not thinking I would be elected but would help the other candidates focus and present themselves better.

I was wrong and a bit stunned when I received the most votes. I reluctantly accepted and during my senior year managed to go by the BSU office almost every day. I appointed fellow students to committees who did a great job. At the end of the school year when I was a senior, we had a BSU banquet in the Magnolia Room. I gave a Janus speech, looking backward and forward. When I sat down the incoming president of the group presented me with an attaché case with my initials on it. As I understand it, neither the end of the year banquet nor a gift were traditional. My experiences with the BSU, besides the banana incident, were very meaningful.

CHAPTER 107

Challenge

My senior year, a group of students headed by Norma Murdock planned for and executed a program sponsored by the College Union titled "Challenge." It was a three-day affair focused on bringing in a variety of speakers to challenge our minds. The two headliners were Dick Gregory, a comedian and civil rights activist, and George Lincoln Rockwell, the head of the American Nazi Party. It was quite a contrast and is probably too controversial to be held on most college campuses today!

Dick Gregory was humorous but pointed in his remarks about segregation, integration, and American society. He challenged everyone to become involved in the civil rights movement and gave excellent reasons for doing so. The audience was moved. George Lincoln Rockwell, who spoke on another day, was paranoid, prejudiced, and troubled in professing what he believed. He was to the right of right and would have been more comfortable and accepted in pre-World War II Germany than in 1966 America. Students and faculty protested his appearance on campus. They walked up and down the aisles of Wait Chapel with black armbands. It was a tense situation but no one disrupted his speech although students shouted obscenities at him when he left and got in his car. No one was changed by his closed-minded, hateful, and anti-Semitic speech and no one signed up to be a Nazi that day.

CHAPTER 108

TP and the Moravians!

TRADITIONS AT "THE FOREST"

When Wake Forest moved to Winston-Salem in 1956 students saw and experienced a lot of red clay on the quad in front of Wait Chapel. It was not aesthetically pleasing so when grass was planted, a tradition followed that everyone would stay off the grass. A low chain railing was put around the quad as a reminder and inhibitor of those who were unaware. On the upper quad, 48 elm trees were planted also. By the time I arrived at Wake, the trees had grown considerably, there was a magnificent canopy, and the grass was as lush as any I have ever seen.

While walking on the grass seldom occurred during the week, the weekends were another matter because that is when most athletic contests occurred. When a Wake Forest team won, especially in football and basketball, not only did students run out on the grass, they toilet papered the trees as well. The TP (toilet paper) tradition started by accident. It had not occurred on the old campus where a bell was rung when there was a victory. Since the bell was not available on the new campus, students took to the trees. TP-ing became a tradition that bonded the campus together. Everyone could participate.

The TP students threw was from their own bathrooms. If a suite was too enthusiastic, the occupants had to borrow from others, go buy a roll or two, or visit nearby restaurants or business establishments when nature called. Monday morning the grounds crew meticulously removed the TP from the elms and usually cut the grass. The campus landscape was pristine again.

A second tradition that became popular slightly later had to do with the Moravians, a German, Protestant religious group that settled the Salem part of Winston-Salem in the mid-1700s. At Christmas time, the Moravians held what they called a Love Feast with sweet milk-laden coffee, freshly baked buns, and beeswax candles. The service was at night and involved servers who would pass the elements to the congregation while traditional Christmas hymns were sung.

The first Moravian Love Feast was held at Wake in December 1966. I will never forget my roommate rushing into the room and saying "You want to go to a Love Feast?" and my instantly replying "Do I?!" The event in Davis Chapel that night was not what I expected. Still, it was meaningful.

These two traditions at Wake Forest were my favorites. Both have evolved since with the University supplying toilet paper to students now and the Love Feast having grown to becoming the largest such celebration of its type in North America.

CHAPTER 109

A Summer Camp Surprise

FORT BRAGG

Although I had three years of high school Junior ROTC and three years of college ROTC, I was not ready for ROTC "camp," i.e., basic training, in between my junior and senior years in college. The reason was more mental than anything else. My brother who had the same ROTC background and was taller (5' 10"), heavier (probably 150 pounds), and much more athletic than me had been dismissed from ROTC summer camp the year before I went because of having dislocated hips as an infant. My family thought the same would happen to me since I had had a more serious case of this malady and been hospitalized longer. With the assumption of being physically rejected, I got a summer job and told my employer that although I had to report to Fort Bragg for ROTC summer camp, I was sure they would be sending me home after the physical and I would be back to work in a few days.

I could not have been more wrong! I drove to North Carolina from Atlanta and stayed with my friend, John Carriker in Kittrell, a small town in the eastern part of the state. The next day we drove down to Fort Bragg and checked in. Soon the process of physical examinations began. I went through each station of being physically inspected. The doctors checked me for everything imaginable. I passed. To make sure there had not been a mistake, I told the last doctors about my hip history and my brother's experience the previous year. He listened and sent me to get x-rays. The process was long and involved a lot of waiting. When I reported back to where the physical exams had been held that day, it was about 8 p.m. The one doctor remaining looked at my x-rays and said flippantly but in all seriousness: "You look like a killer to me." With that, I was pronounced fit for training and around 10 p.m. standing in the back of a deuce and a half, I was driven from the hospital to my barrack.

I was in disbelief and looked out for hours at a yellow porch light that lit the entrance to a building across from the barrack. I finally fell asleep only to be suddenly awakened at 5 a.m. by the First Sergeant in charge of our unit. He was rather loud and his orders contained a number of expletives I will not repeat here. I quickly dressed like the rest of my company and fell out in formation. I was in the Army!

I called my parents at the end of that day with my voice cracking a bit, as I explained what had happened. My dad said he would notify my employer. After the initial rough beginning, I settled down, settled in, and worked hard to be a soldier. I did fine although I found the physical part of basic training difficult . . . and most of basic training was physical! What I liked best about the training was the firing range where I became a Marksman. What I liked least was pull-ups before "mess," aka, food.

The next fall, based on my military science academic classes and my summer camp scores, I was inducted into Scabbard and Blade, the ROTC honor society. Only the top 10% of ROTC class at Wake Forest received this distinction. Later in life, I was installed in the Wake Forest ROTC Hall of Fame and the U. S. Army National ROTC Hall of Fame. I did not deserve either of the last two honors but I graciously and humbly accepted them. I guess summer camp was not so bad after all.

CHAPTER 110

The Good Neighbor House

PATTERSON AVENUE

After basic training was over, I decided that instead of going back to work for six weeks, I would knock off a couple of summer school courses in order to make my senior year at Wake Forest easier. Since I was president of the Baptist Student Union, I figured I should try to be involved in at least one summer activity of the association. An opportunity availed itself immediately. During the spring semester a group of BSU students had moved into a house on Patterson Avenue, approximately two miles from campus. It became the "Good Neighbor House" in a neighborhood of Black and White lower class income family living near a furniture factory downtown. The group had done much good as far as I could tell during the spring by simply helping those around them. However, the original group had now graduated. The house needed a keeper for the rest of the summer. I volunteered.

Living in the house was not a hard task. It required my keeping an open door and a presence in the neighborhood when I was not in class or studying. I would often go play kickball with the kids nearby or invite them into the house for a soft drink or water. At other times, I would chat with my adult neighbors. The house was not air-conditioned and became rather warm but the six weeks I lived there passed quickly.

The Good Neighbor House is no longer standing and the houses around it have been demolished as well. I am glad I lived there although I know my parents were a bit mortified. Patterson Avenue is still changing. The experience changed me and gave me a new perspective on those less fortunate in our society.

CHAPTER 111

The Beers of My Senior Year

I was somewhat naïve and even a bit innocent to the ways of the world when I entered Wake Forest. I grew up in a teetotaling family, i.e., no one drank alcohol. My brother drank beer as a first year student when he went off to college because he joined a fraternity where drinking was prevalent. However, since I was not a member of a fraternity and Russell had never offered to buy me anything alcoholic, I did not know how beer tasted or how much it would affect my behavior. My friends did though. On my 20th birthday, they decided to introduce me to beer. I immediately hated the taste but at their urging and at their expense—they were buying—I consumed a few cans hoping the taste would get better. It did not!

When we arrived back on campus, I was a little woozy. My friends suggested I just lay down for a few minutes. They found a nice place on the grass in front of Wait Chapel where they laid me out Spread Eagle and left. I am not sure how long I was there. Eventually the night patrol officer came along and realized where I lay was not my usual resting spot. He asked a few questions and then helped me to my dorm room. The next morning I had a headache the size of nearby Salem Lake but was none-the-worse-for-wear except for wrinkled clothes. I had learned there was no similarity between beer and sweet tea and that my friends were mischievous.

The second beers of my senior year were not ones I drank but a number of beers I saw consumed at a party the College Union was sponsoring. I was chair of the Small Socials Committee of the Union and planned off campus dances for fellow Deacons. Attendance was usually around a hundred. Besides planning, I paid the band, ordered refreshments, and acquired a chaperone—yes, off campus parties had to be chaperoned in the 1960s! The venue for the December party was the Robert E. Lee Hotel downtown and I found a great band I knew would be a hit. As a chaperone, I persuaded the head of the Baptist Collection in the Z. Smith Reynolds Library to come. I figured he would bring a book and sit in a corner.

All went well for about the first hour or so. Then I noticed my scholarly and introverted chaperone seemed to be having the time of his life out with his wife on the dance floor. In each hand, he had a can of beer. Some of my peers were out dancing with beers too and obviously enjoying more than the music. Uh-oh. I quickly found the source of the happiness, a bartender serving a variety of suds. Not thinking clearly, I wondered if maybe, just maybe, beer could be considered a light refreshment and allowable. To find out, I made a call to one of the deans of the University. When I popped the question, the answer came back with an icy "Certainly not!" Double uh-oh!

There was only one thing to do, stop the flow of liquid gold and try to hide the evidence that the party had gone off the rails. Stopping the flow was easy although not popular. Paying for the damage so I would not be expelled from school was more challenging. First, my peers and the Baptist Collection librarian had consumed hundreds of dollars' worth of alcohol, much more than the price of refreshments in my budget. Second, the laws of North Carolina at the time required the hotel to report alcohol consumption by the bottle and can. I knew what the hotel put on the bill would affect me. With a bit of pleading, I convinced the management to make out a separate Wake Forest tab for me with just three words: "Food and Beverage." The official State of North Carolina information would not be a part of my paperwork.

I have been grateful for many kind acts in my life but the billing the hotel gave me that night is one of those for which I will always be thankful. Without it, I might never have graduated from college and likely would have become either a barista or a booking agent for bands.

CHAPTER 112

Hot Nuts over Spring Break

S pring Break at Wake was supposed to be a time of fun in the sun at the beach, if you could afford it. My senior year, I could not afford much of anything. Funds were low and assignments for the rest of the semester were high. Misery loves company so with a car full of fellow students in the same predicament, I headed for Atlanta during our time off. I would love to say that every night those of us who were home got together and partied. Such was not the case. Mostly, we caught up on sleeping, reading, and studying. To make the time more dreary and unexciting, it rained almost every day.

Traveling back to Winston-Salem with the group, we commiserated about what our time had been like at home. No one had done anything approaching the concept of exciting. We felt ashamed for being so dull but truthfully, we had been. Near South Carolina, on I-85, an event happened that changed our mood. A bus passed us. On its side was a sign that read "The Hot Nuts." In the 1960s, the Hot Nuts were a rather risky, some might say "raunchy," band whose lyrics were unsuitable for anyone but college students who had downed a drink or two. We were a bit excited about seeing the bus and some of its occupants. We waved in delight. Later, after making a pit stop, we were passed by the same bus again.

Back on campus, a newly tanned friend, who looked smug, asked me what I had done over Spring Break. Without hesitating, I replied "I saw the Hot Nuts . . . twice!" His jaw dropped. I smiled. Darkness had turned into light. The interchange made up for the previous week.

CHAPTER 113

Chapel and Nancy Carol

hapel was required at Wake Forest for all undergraduates during most of the 1960s. It took place on Tuesday and Thursday mornings from 11 a.m. to 12 p.m. One of the services was designated as religious; the other was supposed to be secular. Many of my peers did not like either rendition of Chapel but I loved both. The reason: I had been randomly assigned to sit next to Nancy Carol Bost, a cheerleader and one of the prettiest girls on campus. She was as nice as she was beautiful. As luck would have it, she had a boyfriend. "Rats!" Still, she was very pleasant and I enjoyed being that close to someone of her caliber.

I do not remember much of what went on in Chapel except when we were bored we would noisily fold and read newspapers or sleep. Such behavior occurred when we had sermons from visiting ministers who condemned us to hell or tried to save us. The best Chapel services were when we had pep rallies or entertainment, such as music, dance, readings, or other arts. One time some fraternity pledges brought in the University of North Carolina ram they had kidnapped the night before. Another time the Winston-Salem State cheerleaders came over to teach us how to support our athletic teams better by learning a new cheer "What's the matter with the team?" My favorite moment in Chapel, besides every hour I sat next to Nancy Carol, was being tapped into Omicron Delta Kappa, the men's leadership honorary. My regret for that day was having to leave my seat and Nancy Carol and go stand in the front of the student body.

Overall, I am afraid whatever Chapel was supposed to be was mostly wasted on me. I was much too taken with Nancy Carol to have cared.

CHAPTER 114

Swinging and Undue Public Affection

In the 1960s, young women had a number of hurdles to jump—or run around—to go out on a date or leave campus. For instance, at Wake Forest, and most other colleges, when female students checked out of their dorms for an off campus activity they had to fill out a card that detailed where they were going and with whom. To make matters more restrictive yet, they had to return to their dorm at a prescribed hour. In addition, they were not allowed to be too passionate with a date in saying good night for the evening or else they were charged with Undue Public Affection (UPA) and confined to the dorm for two weekends. In other words, you had multiple rules to follow if you were a young woman away at college. On the other hand, young men seemed to have few rules. As long as we did not tear up the campus, get into fights, or stage panty raids, we were considered "good" and no one bothered us.

One of those times I became most aware of the rules women faced was on a date during an extension of dating hours one Saturday night. I did not realize my date still had an hour before she would be considered late checking back into the dorm. I did not want her to think I had not enjoyed the evening or insult her by bringing her back early, so I quickly said as we neared the campus after seeing a movie "Want to try swinging?" In the 1960s "swinging" was a rather risky term. She looked at me askance so I quickly followed up by saying "It'll be fun. The swings are right behind the Chapel." The swings were there as part of a preschool program.

I parked the car near the swings and we probably swung for forty-five minutes. In the excitement of being up in the air, we became a bit affectionate, after which I walked her back to her residence hall, which was only five minutes away. The bright porch lights in front of the dorm, which were the next best thing to floodlights, were on. In saying good night, we did not engage in an UPA like a nearby couple. We had already engaged in DAPA (Duly Appreciated Private Affection). A quick kiss and an "I enjoyed swinging" exchange ended the night. It seemed just right.

CHAPTER 115

When You Are Smiley, Your Signature Says Everything

I flipped a coin to decide if I would major in history or English at Wake Forest. History won and my assigned upper division advisor was Dr. David Smiley, one of the most intriguing and eccentric professors on campus. Dr. Smiley was a somewhat short and round man, who was outwardly friendly and the embodiment of politeness. He often wore a beret and in later years, he was known for riding his bicycle around the upper quad and picking up litter. He was an intriguing lecturer who infused humor, facts, and a touch of sarcasm in his well-prepared and highly entertaining classes. In summary, he was smart, articulate, and somewhat of a character. Everyone knew him or knew of him.

Dr. Smiley's specialty was Southern history. I took two of his classes my senior year, which opened my eyes to who Southerners had been and were now. As my advisor, Dr. Smiley was excellent in helping me figure out my schedule each semester but he had one peculiarity. He would not sign my schedule card if I listed my ROTC class on it. Instead, he would autograph my card with the other classes listed and then insist that I go somewhere out of his sight to fill in the ROTC class. This ritual went on each semester of my junior and senior years. Later I found out why. He had been among the troops landing on the beaches of France during D-Day in World War II. He had fought long and hard in freeing Europe but had seen the horrors of the combat up close. His experiences had made him anti-war. His refusal to sign my registration card was his silent protest.

William Butler Yeats
and Edwin Graves Wilson

I stumbled blindly upon the poetry of William Butler Yeats and one of *Esquire* magazine's Super Professors, Dr. Edwin Graves Wilson my senior year at Wake Forest. Dr. Wilson, besides being a professor, was the Dean of the College. He taught one course each semester. In the fall, he lectured on the romantic poets, e.g., Keats, Wordsworth, Byron, and Shelley. In the spring, it was Blake, Yeats, and Thomas. When I initially heard about Dr. Wilson in the fall semester, it was too late to sign up for his class. My friends who were taking his course raved about it even though they said it was hard and involved a lot of reading and memorization. Multiple recommendations made me vow I would take Wilson's class in the spring and I did.

To say the class was packed would be like saying the Wake Forest campus is beautiful. Dr. Wilson was a spellbinder. His lectures were captivating. He was always well prepared and was truly gifted at holding our attention. Although married with children, his good looks and sophistication made him extremely popular with the women of Wake. The ratio of women to men in his class was 3 to 1—just the opposite of what the college enrollment was.

The literary and artistic talents of William Blake fascinated me. I found the melodious sound of Dillion Thomas's poetry captivating. However, I liked William Butler Yeats best. His interesting life and his ability to express universal emotions in unique and mystic ways drew me to him. Even now, I will sometimes read Yeats. Each time I find something new, different, and exciting.

During a trip to Ireland in 2016, I came upon a display of Yeats's works at the Irish National Library in Dublin. The two hours I spent there passed like two minutes. Dr. Wilson's class enriched my life in ways I am still discovering. It also made me a fan of Irish poetry.

CHAPTER 117

How Can We Lose
When We Are So Sincere?

My undergraduate years at Wake Forest were not bathed in athletic glory. Our major sports teams had mediocre to poor seasons with only men's golf being good. There was little else about which to cheer. Still, that is exactly what most students did. They went to athletic contests and yelled, clapped, stomped, and let our teams know they were there supporting them. One year we even had a cannon that would fire when we scored a touchdown. It was sponsored by a group called 742, which stood for the corresponding letters in the alphabet and had to do with words about what to call a divinity, a structure beavers build, and the Baptists. There was a belief and an optimism in the student body. Even though Wake Forest College teams went into most athletic contests as underdogs, there was a chance they could win. The improbable happened just enough to keep that hope alive. It was like intermittent reinforcement.

My favorite part of the school spirit cycle occurred with the signs put up in The Pit. The women's societies were especially good at painting signs and posting them. Many were humorous, such as the one of Snoopy—a Peanut cartoon character—throwing a football with the words beneath "How can we lose when we are so sincere?" Lose we did—a lot! Sincerity did not translate into ability. Still, it was fun to go to games and occasional victories made it rewarding!

CHAPTER 118

Trying to Smoke

A TRYING EXPERIENCE

I tried three times to start smoking during my senior year at Wake Forest. All three times, I failed—thank goodness! The reason I tried was that smoking in the 1960s seemed to be the epitome of being an adult. Most of the more mature students knew how to smoke whether they did or not. I was hoping to be as laid back and sophisticated!

My first try was with a pack of Camels. The cigarette brand was made in Winston-Salem at Whitaker Park, a mile from the Wake Forest campus. When the breeze was blowing toward the College on cool autumn nights, I could smell the tobacco from the plant. I purchased my pack out of the vending machine in our dorm for twenty-five cents. I then waited for my roommate to leave and lit up. "Cough, cough, cough!" There was an art to smoking and I did not have it at first. Therefore, I kept lighting up, inhaling, coughing a bit, and finally feeling a little sick. I think I had one cigarette left in the pack when I threw it away and aired out the room. For a quarter, I could get a coke, an ice cream cone, or something I enjoyed. I never purchased cigarettes again.

Discouraged but not defeated, I did not give up! I next went to cigars. I told my friends I was going to smoke a cigar every time Wake Forest won a football game. I should have picked another sport for we only won three games each year during both my junior and senior years. I have scientific evidence that you cannot become addicted to cigars with such infrequent wins. Alas, my cigar phase became history.

Despite the fact I was having a hard time smoking, I realized there was still one last behavior where you could burn tobacco and look urbane: a pipe. Therefore, I went out and bought one with some fragrant pipe tobacco to go into the bowl. When I lit up, I thought I was debonair and refined. That was before my friends saw the pipe. Each one, and there must have been a dozen, wanted to look suave and sophisticated, too. Into their mouths the pipe went. I washed the pipe after every episode but after so many scrubbings, it tasted like soap. Hence, I laid it aside and never picked it up again.

I owe part of my health and clean lungs to the effect of smoking a pack of Camel cigarettes, two Wake Forest football teams with bad season records, and friends who mouthed off to me by putting my pipe in their mouths. I am most fortunate.

CHAPTER 119

The Information Desk

TOO MUCH INFORMATION

Although my parents paid my college tuition, I worked some for a part of my spending money. One of those jobs was "manning" the Information Desk, which was right inside Reynolda Hall. My responsibilities were to look alert, sit at the center of the desk, and answer visitors' questions. I was always to look neat and well-groomed and be friendly.

The job was relatively easy and I enjoyed my interactions with those who came to the desk. What I found disconcerting was my supervisor. She was the wife of a faculty member in the English Department and she loved to gossip. When my shift involved meeting her after lunch, I would have to endure 10 or 15 minutes of gossip from her before I was able to slip away. By the time my employment at the information desk ended, I knew everything about everybody who was an adult working for the College. I did not consider that a bonus but it is what I got.

CHAPTER 120

Not By Academics Alone

THE LIBRARY

I loved the Z. Smith Reynolds (ZSR) Library as a student. First, it was architecturally breathtaking. It had classic lines and stood out handsomely. Second, ZSR was spacious. There was a lot of room within the building to either study or simply walk around. On the top two floors was the theatre. On the roof was a coffee shop run by the chaplains where a student could get a Russian tea and a piece of Moravian Sugar Cake. There was room on the roof also to go out on warm nights and gaze at the stars. The third reason I treasured the library was that it gave me employment. I was able to sit at the front desk at night and check books out for students. Often during the day when I came into work, I was assigned to reshelve books. There was nothing romantic about this second task but occasionally I stumbled upon a book I wanted to read.

Finally, the ZSR Library was the perfect place to pick up a date. While the women's dorms had quiet hours, many women studied in the library. It was the social as well as the studious thing to do. One of my friends, Monty, would scan the library floors around 9 p.m. when he was in need of a date. It was systematic. If he did not find someone of interest, he left. If he did find someone he thought might go out with him, he approached her. We all admired him for his boldness.

While I only ended up getting a few dates from my library experience, I eventually married a librarian. I checked her out and never returned her.

CHAPTER 121

The Pit before Fresh Food

'He has redeemed my soul from going to the pit,
And my life shall see the light.' Job 33:28

I am not sure how the main dining facility at Wake Forest came to be called "The Pit." Perhaps, it was because it was on the bottom floor of Reynolda Hall and coming from what is now Hearn Plaza, people had to descend to it by taking the stairs, two sets of which were there in the late 1960s but have now been covered up. There is also the theory that the food was bad and "the pits" in terms of taste. Connected with that theory is the idea found in the Book of Job that because the food was not good, students prayed for another source of nourishment and hoped to see the light of another cuisine.

However, for a full time student who lived on campus, it was all but impossible to skip The Pit, which is now the Fresh Food Company. There were only two other places to eat on campus, not counting the vending machines. They were the Soda Shop, which is now where Global Studies is located, and the Magnolia Room, which only served meals at night by candlelight. Unless students had a car and wanted to go off campus to eat, they were stuck with Pit food.

Most students, including me, had a meal plan. Every time we ate in The Pit, we would go through one of two lines that served the same entrees. After getting our food, the cashier would ring up whether the meal was breakfast, lunch, or dinner. Breakfast was standard with the usual items a person would find at any breakfast bar. Lunch and dinner varied with most often a choice of meats, vegetables, and desserts. We did not worry about what is now known as "the Freshman 15." No one gained weight on Pit food!

With all of the choices available on the Wake Forest campus today, it is interesting to look back on The Pit from the 1960s. Sometimes we would destroy the food we did not eat so it could not be served later, which was known to happen. Most often, we ate what we could or what we wanted and surrendered to the inevitable. To protest was all but hopeless and to starve was not an option.

CHAPTER 122

Box 6567

My post office mailbox, in the days before email, was 6567. It was located where all the other mailboxes on campus were, in what is now Zick's below Poteat Residence Hall on Hearn Plaza. Instead of pizza or flatbread, which is the main cuisine of Zick's, the space contained a post office and campus mailboxes full of stamped envelopes with letters. Mail was tangible with handwritten messages on paper. A few epistles were perfumed; most were not. Some contained checks but the majority just contained words.

My father was especially good at writing once a week but my mother wrote me, too. Both had superb handwriting. My penmanship on the other hand started with another "s" word that rhymes with jalopy—"sloppy." I tried to write legibly but my cursive seemed cursed.

Like many Wake Forest students, part of my week was spent writing home and like most of my peers, I valued getting mail, especially before Chapel when there was time to read and digest it. Looking back, I find it ironic that I entered Wake Forest in '65 and graduated in '67. My mailbox—6567—had my numbers even before I arrived!

A Final Paper

GETTING BY WITH
WIDE MARGINS AND MODIFIERS

After spending two action packed years at Wake Forest, the time to prepare for commencement came. I had exams to pass and papers to complete in my finals week. While I did not like exams, I was not too worried about them. Papers were usually not a problem either but I had not had time to write my 10 page paper for Cultural Anthropology. I literally had a weekend to complete it.

My time at Wake was in the B.C.—before computers! I had to go to the library, which closed at 5 p.m. on Saturdays and did not open until noon on Sundays to find sources. I had a challenge before me not only because of the library hours but because most of my resources were going to have to come from books which I had yet to discover. I was panicked! When I turned my final paper in on Monday, after typing most of Sunday night, it had wide margins and a lot of adjectives and adverbs.

I will never know what grade my paper received because it was never returned. I managed to get a B for the course, made the Dean's List, and with Cultural Anthropology out of the way, I was eligible to graduate. With mixed feelings, I packed up my "stuff," and headed home to spend a few restful, non-academic days recuperating before driving back with my parents for commencement.

CHAPTER 124

Commencement and Good-bye

O ne of the nicest aspects of the commencement weekend were house visits with several of my professors who invited graduates and their parents in for snacks and chat after the bachelorette sermon on Sunday night. I think my parents were impressed that the professors were so welcoming and warm. It left a good feeling in my heart as well.

On Monday morning, the commencement ceremony on the Quad went off without a hitch. The speaker and his message were not impressive but the announcement that Wake Forest was transitioning from a college to a university was. After the ceremony ended. I turned in my robe, quickly changed into my Army uniform, and was commissioned in the ROTC department headquarters in the basement of Reynolds Gym. From there, I took my diploma to McNabb Studio in Davis Dorm where Tommy McNabb, the owner, framed it while my parents and I ate lunch in The Pit.

The surprise of the day happened at lunch when Rose, a young woman I dated once—like one time—and had become friends with since, came up to me and gave me a present. It was a book titled *I Like You*, a quick and humorous read. I had not thought of saying "good-bye" to Rose before leaving so I was completely thrown off guard. Nevertheless, I expressed my gratitude, collected my now framed diploma and headed back to Decatur with my folks. We had casual conversation along the way and on reaching home, I thanked my parents for affording me the privilege of a college education and told them someday I would like to return to Wake Forest. Twenty-three years and three additional degrees later, it happened.

Epilogue

THE REST OF THE STORY

The late Paul Harvey, a radio news reporter and commentator, used to highlight the last part of his program by saying "And now for the rest of the story." He would then launch into details of human interest stories that were not apparent or had not been reported.

The purpose of this book has not been to report the rest of the story, i.e., to provide an autobiographical sketch of my life past the age of 21 when I finished college. That story has been told in a number of other publications, which I am listing at the end of this book. If you are interested, please peruse. If you do not wish to examine these publications or simply want a quick overview of my life from the fall of 1967 to the fall of 2019, I have provided a timeline that gives you a few highlights and lowlights. Whichever you chose, I hope you have enjoyed the stories in this book.

How we begin our lives is not necessarily how we live them or where we end up. Becoming is evolutionary and sometimes revolutionary. We have free will and are not destined to live in our past. The unpredictable and happenstance mix with plans, dreams, and talents in a spirited intermingling of our choices, our resilience, and our grit.

Timeline from the Fall of 1967 to the Fall of 2019

1967   After graduating from Wake Forest in the spring, I take a course in German at Emory and begin studying religion at WFU in the fall. The material I am assigned to read is dry and tedious. I take more German because of influence of German scholars on theology. I think my professors are dull and uninspiring. Oh my! Still, I apply to divinity schools—Princeton, Vanderbilt, Southern, and Yale. I choose Yale. I can spell it!

1968   I take part in Civil Rights march/activities at Wake Forest after the death of Martin Luther King, Jr. in April. I start Yale Divinity School in the fall. I am introduced to a harsher environment but an extraordinary learning milieu.

1969   I decide not to become a minister. It does not feel right. However, I finish Yale and take courses all over the University. Before graduation I break my right ankle playing intramural volleyball.

1970   I participate in anti-war marches in Washington and New Haven and go see my senator, Herman Talmadge, as a part of the process. I graduate from Yale and begin counselor education program at Wake Forest. I become engaged to J.

1971   I graduate from WFU counseling program and take first job in rural Rockingham County (NC) at the mental health center in Wentworth. I move to Reidsville (NC).

1972   My engagement to J is broken. I blame myself for letting outside inter-
        ference get in the way of good decision making and listening to my feel-
        ings. As a result, I have rumination depression that lasts for years. I have
        a dream where my ancestors come and lift me up as I struggle. The dream
        gives me strength and helps me make it through this hard time. I make my
        first professional presentation in Hawaii at the American Psychological
        Association (APA) Conference with my counseling mentor, Tom Elmore.

1973   I report to Fort Lee, Virginia, for active-duty-for-training in the Army
        Quartermaster Corps. I return to the mental health center after discharge.
        Wes Hood, another WFU mentor, takes my place when I am away. I move
        to Greensboro (NC) and join the singles group at the First Baptist Church.

1974   I begin taking night courses at UNCG as well as working. I have first
        professional American Counseling Association (ACA) publication—a
        poem—in their flagship journal.

1975   I stay physically active playing tennis and dating as well as stay mentally
        active taking courses in counseling, psychology, and family life/human
        development at UNCG as I begin a Ph.D.

1976   I begin work at as instructor of psychology at Rockingham Community
        College (RCC) in Wentworth, NC, teaching introduction to psychology,
        developmental psychology, and abnormal psychology. I self-publish a
        thin book of poetry, *Reality Sits in a Green-Cushioned Chair*.

1977   I receive a Ph.D. from UNCG and cash in my life insurance policy to make
        a down payment on a house in Greensboro. I become chair of the Greens-
        boro Single Living Committee for the Greensboro Family Life Council.

1978   Grandmother Gladding dies at the age of 94. I go to Richmond for the
        funeral. I break my right ankle again playing tennis. I learn to drive with
        my left foot to get to work. I am promoted to Captain and receive an hon-
        orable discharge from the Army. I join the singles group at the First Pres-
        byterian Church.

1979   I take a semester unpaid leave from the community college to complete
        an 18-semester hour post doctorate in psychology at UNCG during the
        summer and fall and begin a process of applying for positions in coun-
        selor education. I am appointed to the editorial board of *Personnel and
        Guidance Journal*, the flagship journal of ACA. I take up sailing. I meet Art

Lerner from California at an APA conference after I quote him during a presentation. He becomes a friend and mentor.

1980   I am rejected for a counselor education position at Wake Forest. I apply to almost 200 other positions. I buy a sheltie with help from my sister and name him "Eli." My father's business fails. I become closer to him and identify more with the Gladdings through talks with him over the next 14 years. I am selected by students at RCC to be their commencement speaker.

1981   I accept a position as an assistant professor of counselor education at Fairfield University. My singles group at First Presbyterian throw a surprise sendoff party for me the last Saturday night I am in Greensboro. It is a bittersweet way to depart, bitter because I am moving, sweet because of what my friends have done to show they care. I move to Milford, Connecticut where I teach 12 different courses during my tenure at Fairfield in a conflictual department. I am initially socially isolated and pretend I am a captive/hostage in a foreign country. I write to "stay alive" and have success publishing in ACA journals. I am selected again by students at RCC to be their commencement speaker. It is the highlight of my first year in Connecticut.

1982   I become a "certified counselor" and "mental health counselor" through the National Board for Certified Counselors. My teaching and writing go well. I renew my friendship with Jim Chapman from Wake Forest days. He is a minister in Glastonbury.

1983   I meet Claire Helena Tillson, a school librarian, from Bridgeport, CT and begin a dating relationship. I am turned down for promotion to associate professor at Fairfield. I co-edit a book on marriage and family therapy with Barbara Okun.

1984   I am promoted to associate professor at Fairfield but leave and take a position at the University of Alabama-Birmingham (UAB) and enter private practice as a counselor simultaneously. It is an easy transition because of a good department chair, Jim Davidson.

1985   I become engaged to Claire. I set up a marriage and family counseling program at UAB where I teach 13 different courses during my tenure there. I have a book proposal turned down by Brooks Cole but become newsletter editor for the Association for Specialists in Group Work.

1986   Claire and I marry in Davis Chapel on the Wake Forest campus May 24. Jim Chapman officiates. Claire moves to Birmingham July 4th and becomes pregnant in late July. I have a book proposal accepted by Merrill Education.

1987   Son, Benjamin Templeman Gladding, is born, April 21st; I am promoted to full professor at UAB and finish my 40th journal article. I receive the outstanding publication award from Association of Humanistic Counseling (AHC). I organize and direct a national conference on poetry therapy in Birmingham at the request of Art Lerner. Claire goes to work again as a school librarian.

1988   Son, Nathaniel Tillson Gladding, is born November 13th. He shares the same month/day as my Grandmother Templeman aka, Pal, "Lucky 13." Claire stops working to become a full-time mother. I become editor of the *Journal for Specialists in Group Work (JSGW)*. My first book is published— *Counseling: A Comprehensive Profession*.

1989   Claire and I buy a new house in Birmingham. I am elected president of Chi Sigma Iota, counseling honor society international, and am appointed to Alabama Board of Examiners of Professional Counselors. I receive a grant and make my first film: *Uses of Poetry and Metaphor in Counseling*. My mother suffers a massive heart attack while Samuel Templeman II, her brother and my favorite uncle, dies. I am a pallbearer.

1990   I take a position as assistant to the president of Wake Forest and we move to Winston-Salem NC. We buy a house about 5 miles from campus and put up swings, a slide, and install a sandbox and other playground equipment in the backyard for the boys. The last vestiges of my rumination depression end through counseling. I begin teaching graduate counseling courses and volunteer in the counseling center as well.

1991   Son, Timothy Huntington Gladding, is born on March 4th. Unfortunately he inherits Brachydactyly Type C syndrome from my side of the family and has dislocated hips and missing digits in fingers. He has operations and is put in a body cast beginning October 31st. He has to be re-circumcised as well. Our household is hectic with three children in it under age five. My second book is published—*Group Work*.

1992   My third book, *Creative Arts in Counseling*, is published. I am elected president of Southern Association for Counselor Education and Supervision

---

(SACES). I resign as *JSGW* editor. I am chosen to go to Japan for two weeks as part of a North Carolina leadership group. I start a five-year stint of representing WFU on the executive board of the North Carolina Association of Independent Colleges and Universities. Timothy gets out of body cast on Martin Luther King's holiday. We celebrate King and Tim simultaneously with cake.

1993   Shirley Ratliff, an older UAB counseling student, sets up a scholarship in my name at Wake Forest. It is for students from Alabama since that is her home. I receive the outstanding publication award in counselor education from the Association of Counselor Education and Supervision (ACES). Ben begins kindergarten.

1994   I am elected president of Association for Specialists in Group Work (ASGW). My father dies suddenly in April at age 84. I am greatly saddened. Life is hectic at home with our 7, 5, and 3 year old boys.

1995   My fourth book, *Family Therapy*, is published. I become interim chair of Wake Forest University Department of Religion. I am chosen as the faculty member to go with WFU City of Joy scholars—12 undergraduates—to Calcutta to work with Mother Teresa for three weeks. We live as close to poverty as possible. Everyone gets sick but works hard. I am invited to speak at University of Lund in Sweden—my first overseas presentation. Nate begins kindergarten.

1996   I become the director of the counselor education program and teach a first year seminar on leadership with Wake Forest President Thomas K. Hearn. I become president of Association for Counselor Education and Supervision (ACES) and publish two book revisions, too. I become a Fellow in ASGW. I begin jogging again and chair the staff/parish committee at our church for two years.

1997   I become a scout leader and soccer coach for Tim and Nate. We put up a basketball goal on the side of the driveway and we all shoot baskets. I publish my fifth book *Community Counseling* and receive the Chi Sigma Iota Sweeney professional leadership award. Eli, our dog, dies at age 16. I keynote the European ACA counseling conference in Germany. Tim begins kindergarten and Claire has more time. My mother's health declines and she starts using a walker. I stop jogging because my hips hurt. I take Claire on a WFU basketball trip to Salt Lake City.

1998   I become associate provost at WFU, managing seven offices: admissions, financial aid, institutional research, the Secrest Artists Series, international studies, research and sponsored programs, and the registrar. I have to terminate the registrar. I publish more book revisions and journal articles. I receive the Sweeney counseling leader in residency award from Ohio University. My friend Art Lerner dies. I buy another sheltie for the boys—a female, Maggie. Ben becomes a Boy Scout. I take Ben to see Civil War sites—a 5th grade graduation trip. Professional and family life is hectic.

1999   I hire a new registrar and manage an enrollment crisis. I become overseer of WFDD, the public radio station at WFU, after a scandal. I accept the ACES Robert Frank outstanding program award for WFU counseling program and receive an award recognition from ACES for leadership and the ASGW eminent career award. I write sixth book, *The Counseling Dictionary*. I take Claire on a WFU trip to Vienna, Austria. Claire volunteers to do Math Super Stars at Sherwood Elementary School. Tim suffers a serious facial injury when we vacation at the beach.

2000   I publish 4th edition of *Counseling: A Comprehensive Profession* and my 45th poem in a refereed counseling journal. I am inducted into the WFU ROTC Hall of Fame. I am also selected as a member of the Chi Sigma Iota Academy of Leaders for Excellence. In addition, I co-chair the Year of Ethics and Honor for the University. My mother dies at age 89 in August two months short of her 90th birthday. We drive to Connecticut to celebrate Claire's mother's 90th birthday in December. Nate and Ben are active in Boy Scouts and Tim in Cub Scouts. All the boys play Optimist soccer. I take Nate on 5th grade graduation trip to Washington, D.C. and take family to Vienna where I teach the Vienna Theorists course.

2001   Claire continues volunteering, especially with the Forsyth County Library. I continue to write but give up my home office to Tim so he can have his own room. I volunteer with the Red Cross and work as a mental health counselor in New York City two weeks after the World Trade Center attack on 9/11. Later in October, I take the family to NYC where we are in a taxi accident and anthrax scare. As a family, we are featured in a picture in *Newsweek* and Claire makes the front page of national Canadian paper, *The Globe and Mail*. I receive the Ella Stevens Barrett Leadership Award from the North Carolina Counseling Association. The boys keep Claire and me busy with scouts, band, soccer, homework, and more. Ben graduates from middle school with a number of honors and makes a good adjustment to high school thanks to marching band. Nate wins a minor part in school play "Shenandoah." Tim is small but popular with his peers and is elected co-president of his class. He brings home a kitten—"Frisky Mittens."

2002   I am passed over for an interview for the provost position and a new provost is hired. I think the process unfair but stay on as associate provost and contemplate going back to the faculty. I decide to run for the American Counseling Association (ACA) president and continue to write. I am on the road a lot, including Japan, with speaking engagements. Claire's brother, Tom, dies unexpectedly and we go to Connecticut for the funeral. I begin to take more time off to be with the family. I take Tim on 5th grade graduation trip to "bike the sites" in Washington, DC and to see Williamsburg. I take Claire on short summer trips to see Atlantic Coast Conference schools and to spend time together.

2003   I serve as president of Leadership Winston-Salem and win ACA presidency. I invest more in the counselor education program and in my teaching. I guide the program in forming its own department, separate from Education, and become chair. I continue to publish more books and articles while traveling for ACA to D.C. a lot. I get ready to move from president-elect to president of ACA. At the same time, I begin to try to help Ben with college selection. Ben gets driver's license and has a wreck. We go as a family to Disneyworld and to Sunset Beach for vacations. I try to become more family oriented while simultaneously stepping up to take on more responsibilities in the Provost office when the president takes a leave because of a brain tumor.

2004   I begin my term as president of ACA in June and am on the road and in a plane a lot keynoting 22 state counseling conferences. I run the ACA Governing Council and invite Irvin Yalom to be ACA keynote speaker at our conference. I promote creativity in counseling and continue to write. I set up a new scholarly exchange program between Wake Forest and Kansai Gaidai University in Japan. The 1st edition of *Becoming a Counselor* is published. Nate graduates from middle school. Ben begins flying lessons, goes to Governor's School, and becomes an Eagle Scout. All the boys make First Chair at All State in their music divisions—euphonium (Ben & Tim), oboe (Nate).

2005   I preside over the ACA Convention in Atlanta—biggest in more than a decade—Yalom is a hit. I publish 3rd edition of *Counseling as an Art* and 1st edition of *Counseling Theories*. My first book on counseling is translated into Polish. It will later be translated into a dozen languages including Chinese and Russian. I am inducted into the UAB Counselor Education Hall of Fame. Tim begins acting and graduates from middle school. Ben graduates from high school and starts Furman. Nate becomes an Eagle Scout. Claire's mother dies and we go to Connecticut for the funeral. I take the family to Hawaii for a convention/vacation.

2006   Claire volunteers as a tutor at Old Town elementary school. I keynote the International Association of Counselling Convention in Brisbane, Australia. Claire goes with me. I lead a delegation of 66 counselors to South Africa for two weeks. My work in the Provost Office is fulfilling but I become more involved in counseling and set up a dual degree program between the Department of Counseling and the Divinity School. I publish the 2nd edition of *The Counseling Dictionary*. The Association for Creativity in Counseling (ACC) presents me with a lifetime achievement award. Tim starts excelling in drama, *Pippin*, while Nate and Tim excel in music—oboe & euphonium. Both are in the high school marching band. Tim becomes the third of the Gladding boys to receive the Eagle Scout award. Nate goes to Governor's School.

2007   I audit counseling programs in Malaysia and publish 4th edition of *Family Therapy* as well as make a film on becoming a creative counselor. Claire continues volunteering. I leave the Provost Office and return to the Department of Counseling. I turn down an offer to become Provost at a nearby college. I work for the Red Cross as a mental health counselor after the Virginia Tech shootings and begin counseling on a very limited basis with CareNet of the Triad—a part of the medical school. I am elected an ACA Fellow, receive the ACA Gilbert & Kathleen Wrenn Award for a Humanitarian and Caring Person, receive the Humanitarian Award from the Association for Spiritual, Ethical, and Religious Values in Counseling (ASERVIC), and ACA Foundation's Bridgebuilder Award. Nate graduates high school from the University of North Carolina School of the Arts (UNCSA). Ben transfers to Wake Forest—joins a fraternity and finds a girlfriend. Nate starts WFU. Tim goes to Governor's School and stars in school plays.

2008   The 5th edition of *Group Work* is published. I am appointed to the North Carolina Board of Licensed Professional Counselors and serve in this position until 2014. The Association for Creativity in Counseling (ACC) names an award in my honor emphasizing inspiration and motivation and ACES presents me with an award for counselor advocacy. Nate becomes addicted to computers, drops out of WFU. He begins working for Five Guys. Ben spends fall semester in Dijon, France, where Claire & I visit him in Paris. Tim spends summer at Interlochen Music Camp in Michigan; he polishes his skills on the euphonium, and starts senior year at UNCSA. I put up Bluebird boxes and become somewhat of a birder.

2009   Claire transitions from volunteering to babysit for daughter of a friend. Ben and Nate return home. No empty nest. I have 42 radiation treatments for prostate cancer and am selected for a sabbatical during the fall semester. The Department of Counseling experiences conflict with the administration over money and programs. The 2nd edition of *Becoming a Counselor* and 6th edition of *Counseling* are published. I make a film on spirituality and counseling with Michele Kielty. Tim graduates from UNCSA and begins Yale. Ben graduates from WFU and is hired as a temporary by Volvo because of his fluency in French. Nate continues to be non-productive at WFU after going back—drops out again.

2010   Claire finishes one babysitting job and picks up another. I am appointed as a Fulbright Specialist in Turkey and have an enriching though exhausting experience. Claire joins me for the last week and we tour. I finish 4th edition of *The Creative Arts in Counseling* and the 6th edition of *Groups*. I also teach at Johns Hopkins during the summer, chair the ACA Foundation, and am president of American Association of State Counseling Boards. The ACA names its "unsung heroes" awards after me. I receive the ACA Arthur A. Hitchcock Distinguished Professional Service Award and the International Association of Marriage and Family Counselors research award. Nate starts job with Goodwill and is non-productive until the summer when he takes two communication courses at Wake and makes B's. Ben continues with Volvo and is accepted to teach English in France starting in September. Tim finishes 1st year at Yale and returns for his sophomore year after getting into Glee Club and the Red Hot Poker comedy group.

2011 Claire and I celebrate our 25th wedding anniversary and go to Yellowstone after I speak at BYU-Idaho. I set up a college scholarship in Claire's honor for graduates of the Winston-Salem Schools. I teach in Vienna at the Flow House and keynote the Mexican Counseling Conference. I receive the ACA David K. Brooks, Jr. Distinguished Mentor Award. In late December, I have emergency surgery for an intestinal blockage. Ben teaches for a second year in France. Nate begins work as a barista at Mudhouse Coffee in Charlottesville. Tim plays in the Yale Marching Band. In the summer, he tours Europe with the Glee Club then digs in Turkey.

2012 I rehabilitate from surgery during much of the spring of 2012. An abdominal hernia develops and I have abdominal reconstruction surgery in mid-December 2012. Ouch! I am able to recover in time for the start of the 2013 spring term. The Department of Counseling now has 14 faculty. I make a film on family counseling. Ben, back from France, works for Lenovo. Nate continues as a barista at the Mudhouse. Tim takes a gap year from Yale. Claire continues to volunteer. Maggie, our Sheltie, dies.

2013 I continue serving on the state licensure board for counselors, chair the Department of Counseling at Wake Forest, and continue giving workshops and keynotes for counseling associations and colleges. I also chair the WFU Library Committee and serve as a Faculty Fellow in Babcock Residence Hall through 2016. I receive a second Fulbright Specialist grant, this time to China and teach for a month at Minnan Normal University in Zhangzhou. Claire and I tour Shanghai, Beijing, and Xi'an afterward. I set up a scholarship at Decatur High School in memory of my parents. Claire returns to babysittng. Ben starts his master's degree in education at Wake Forest and begins dating Sara Chisesi. Nate continues as a coffee barista at the Mudhouse in Charlottesville. Tim goes back to Yale.

2014 Claire and I go to Maui for 5 days before ACA Conference in Honolulu. We bike 23 miles down the Haleakalā Crater. I am selected to give the Hubert McNeill Poteat Lecture at Wake Forest. I am also invited to give the keynote at the Philippine Guidance & Counseling Conference. We visit Corregidor. I win the Nathan and Julie Hatch Prize for Academic Excellence for a week of study at Oxford, where I research humor. We take another week and visit the sites of London plus Canterbury, Stonehenge, Dover, Leeds Castle, etc. Next, we take a 10-day cruise to Alaska. Whew! Claire has her gall bladder out after which I teach in Singapore. I receive the

"Distinguished Alumni Award" from the UNCG School of Health & Human Sciences. I set up a departmental fund afterwards in appreciation. Tim works as a barista in New York as does Nate in Charlottesville. Ben becomes a "Double Deacon" by finishing his master's degree. Ben proposes to Sara in France during the Christmas season and they plan a wedding.

2015   I have a hip replacement and finish a four-year term in the WFU faculty senate. Claire serves on the church's Staff/Parish Committee and grows Zinnias. I return to Singapore to teach. A 1990s film on cognitive counseling with Jan Holden is re-released. I make another film on spirituality and counseling with Geri Miller. Tim and Nate move back home and start the fall semester at UNCG and Guilford Tech Community College (GTCC) respectively. They move to Greensboro. Ben & Sara marry December 28th at Davis Chapel at Wake Forest where Claire & I married.

2016   We celebrate our 30th wedding anniversary. I commission composition "This is Love" by Dan Locklair in celebration of the occasion. I complete Volume 6 of the *History of Wake Forest University* after 9 years and publish a book of poetry: *Reflections: 101 Poems*. I am inducted into the national Army ROTC Hall of Fame and we go to Fort Knox for the ceremony. I also give workshops in Kuala Lumpur, Malaysia, and Singapore, keynote the North Dakota Counseling Conference (my 50th state), receive the ACA President's Award in Montreal, set up a scholarship at Yale Divinity School, and make an instructional film on group counseling from a live demonstration.

2017   I become president-elect of the International Association for Marriage & Family Counselors (IAMFC) and chair the WFU Online Education Committee. New editions of *Clinical Mental Health Counseling* and the *Counseling Dictionary* are published. Claire and I set up a fund to fight childhood hunger through the Winston-Salem Foundation. I make a film on creativity in counseling for the Australian Mental Health Academy and a film on spirituality in counseling. Claire starts volunteering at the UNC School of the Arts.

2018   Claire breaks a bone in her leg near her knee while skiing. She is confined to bed for over 3 months and has rehabilitation for another 3 months. I receive the Kenyon Family Faculty Fellowship from Wake Forest and teach 16 first year students in Copenhagen during the fall; it goes well until I break my kneecap two days before returning to the

States. Nate studies in Indonesia, graduates from UNCG with a major in geography, and begins working for the Forsyth County Board of Elections. Tim starts working for a local music store, one requirement short of graduating from UNCG. Ben & Sara move to Casablanca to begin teaching French in an international school.

2019   I publish a new book with a Canadian, Kevin Alderson, *Choosing the Right Counselor for You* and publish the 8th edition of *Groups*. I receive the Excellence in Advising Award from Wake Forest and endow a mental health workshop series in the Department of Counseling. I become a faculty fellow in Luter Residence Hall and the faculty advisor to Alpha Phi Omega (service fraternity) one of the largest groups on the Wake Forest campus. Claire and I set up an athletic scholarship at Wake Forest. We visit Ben and Sara in Casablanca, Morocco, after the birth of their first child, Leo— our first grandchild. We also visit Spain for a couple of days. I finish an animated film—*Adventures in Mental Health* and write a memoir about my first 21 years of life, *Off the Courthouse Square*. My 90th refereed journal article is published. The emphasis is scriptotherapy. I am invited to keynote an international conference in Qatar, my 30th country.

Publications about My Adult Life in Descending Chronological Order

Gladding, S. T. (2019). From Ages 27 to 72: Career and personal development of a productive counselor over the life span. *Adultspan Journal*, 18, 17–26.

Gladding, S. T. (2016). *Reflections: 101 Poems*. Winston-Salem, NC: Library Partners Press.

Donovan, K. A., & Weigel, D. J. (2015). Samuel T. Gladding: A consistent and creative voice in the field of marriage, couple, and family counseling. *The Family Journal*, 23, 201–208.

Henderson, D. A., & Montplaisir, B. F. (2013). From good to great: Examining exemplary counselor development. *Journal of Counseling & Development*, 91, 336–342.

Gladding, S. T. (2010). Facing mortality: Living with cancer. In M. Trotter-Mathison, J. M. Koch, S. Sanger, & T. M. Skovholt (Eds.) *Voices from the Field: Defining Moments in Counselor and Therapist Development* (pp. 242–245). New York: Routledge.

Gladding, S. T. (2009). *Becoming a counselor: The light, the bright, and the serious* (2nd ed.). Alexandria, VA: American Counseling Association.

Haight, M. G., & Shaughnessy, M. F. (2006). An interview with Samuel T. Gladding: Thoughts on becoming a counselor. *Journal of Counseling & Development*, 84(1), 114–119.

Gladding, S. T. (2005). Accentuating the positives. In R. K. Conyne & F. Bemak (Eds.) *Journeys to Professional Excellence: Lessons from leading counselor educators and practitioners* (pp. 19–31). Alexandria, VA: American Counseling Association.

Rosenthal, H. (2002). Samuel T. Gladding on creativity. *Journal of Clinical Activities, Assignments & Handouts in Psychotherapy Practice*, 2, 23–33.

Gladding, S. T. (1999). The faceless nature of racism: A counselor's journey. *Journal of Humanistic Education and Development*, 37, 182–187.

Campbell, L. (1996) Samuel T. Gladding: A sense of self in the group. *The Journal for Specialists in Group Work*, 21, 69–80.

Gladding, S. T. (1990). Becoming a family therapist: An indirect encounter with "Sal." *Contemporary Family Therapy*, 12, 245–247.

Gladding, S. T. (1988). Involuntary isolation: A counselor's dilemma. *Journal of Counseling & Development*, 67(2), 116.

About the Author

S AMUEL T. GLADDING is a story-teller, a mental health counselor, a past president of the American Counseling Association, and a professor in the Department of Counseling at Wake Forest University in Winston-Salem, North Carolina. He has written numerous books, professional articles, poetry, and even produced films. This book recounts stories of his youth, up to age 21.

Made in the USA
Monee, IL
13 January 2020